PHILIPS

A STUDY OF THE CORPORATE MANAGEMENT OF DESIGN

JOHN HESKETT

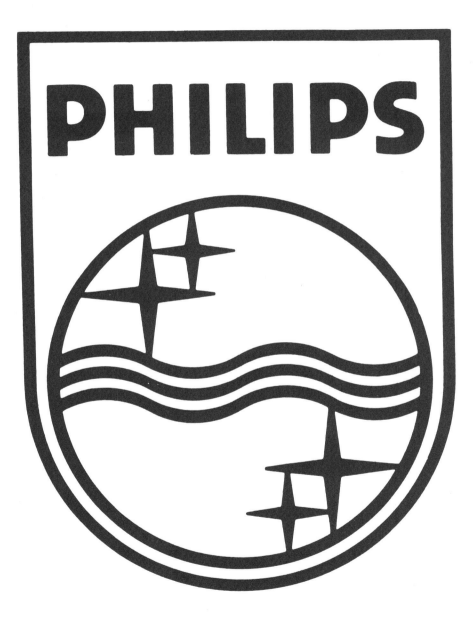

PHILIPS

RIZZOLI INC, NEW YORK

First published in the United States of America in 1989 by
Rizzoli International Publications Inc,
597 Fifth Avenue, New York, NY 10017.

Copyright © John Heskett, 1989

First published in Great Britain by Trefoil Publications, Ltd.
in 1989
Designed by Elizabeth Van Amerongen

ISBN 0-8478-1040-2

LC 88-43426

Printed and bound in Italy by Graphicom srl.

Editor's Introduction

The subject of design management is a current preoccupation in manufacturing industry, and for good reason. The growth of global markets, the expansion of specialized market segments and advances in technology have made it abundantly clear that design is a key tool in industry's armoury to ensure consumer satisfaction, to remain competitive, and to keep market share. The aim of this series is the development of greater design awareness among manufacturers, and the explanation of the values of design management and design management skills into industry. The opportunity presented to study frankly and in detail how the design function operates and how design decisions are made in a management context, must be of inestimable value in the development of a greater consciousness of the importance and relevance of design management.

In planning this series of books with Trefoil, I identified a number of criteria for the inclusion of companies. Among these were that companies should be successful, international, and design-conscious. In addition, the design management function should play a high profile role in the activity of the company. The pages that follow show how Philips has moved towards this goal. Products such as the Tracer shaver and the Roller Radio show Philips moving into new market areas, while initiatives such as the Philips Electronic Office System show how the company has extended its competences into new product ranges. Among all others, the Platinum project, for a new ultrasound medical scanner, shows how the involvment of a designer in product development at an early stage in consultation with potential users can produce excellent and worthwhile results.

This book is necessarily only a partial study of the whole activity of an international giant such as Philips. The reader who hopes to find here an account of Philips' dominant role in the development of new technologies such as compact disc and video disc may be disappointed, but in its palce he will learn much about how Philips has created strength in design in recent years to match the company's strength in research and development.

The companion volume in the series is on Olivetti, where a different design tradition and more cohesive product range provides an equally important example. Further volumes are in preparation. It is our hope that the series will represent a major contibution to the debate on the value and relevance of design management today and tomorrow.

John Heskett

Preface

The subject of design management is of relatively recent origin, but within the last ten years it has come to occupy the attention of many in government, business management and in education as well as in the design profession. The reason is fundamentally simple. Industrial design and graphic design are capable of crucial contributions in making the products we use in every day life better – more satisfactory and more convenient. In a highly competitive world, where there are few obvious differences in technical quality to help distinguish one product from another, it is the perceptible characteristics of products to which consumers and users generally turn. These may be superficial tricks or visual 'features', the visual equivalent of the 'bells and whistles' concept beloved of some marketing men, a gimmick to attract at the point of purchase with little substance thereafter. Or they may be something more substantial, an expression of a sense of quality. The concept of quality is not an absolute: it can take many forms, and requires the creative contribution of many disciplines in addition to that of design. However, if perceived by consumers, and confirmed in their daily use a products, the concept of quality can create a powerful bond of confidence between consumers and producers. A reputation for quality of that kind is one of the most effective competitive advantages available to manufacturers.

Industrial designers are trained to think of how technology is made available, accessible and comprehensible to the general public. Their abilities shape the tangible world we inhabit, and at drawing boards and in workshops across the world, they are anticipating and creating the future physical world. They are capable of both approaches set out above, though my experience is that most designers prefer the latter. What they are able to achieve, however, is entirely dependent upon the calibre and policies of the management under which they serve. It does not matter how talented designers, as individuals or as a group, may be, whether they are working as outside consultants or as direct employees. Unless they are given the opportunity to work with other disciplines involved in the process of product development on a basis of parity, in a company which has an ideal of quality in its products and services for its customers, there is little hope of them realizing their abilities and making the contribution of which they are capable.

Comparatively few companies have a long tradition of employing industrial design in the modern sense and changing entrenched attitudes towards design is not easy. Some still think in terms of styling, a process in which decorative artists add a finishing touch, for example in terms of colour or surface treatment, to a product concept, without being really involved in substantial decisions about the nature of products. Others share the marketing oriented approach of the French/American designer, Raymond Loewy: 'It's good design if it sells'. Still other companies have a strong engineering tradition and belief if a product works well, that is enough. Studies of the competition in any contemporary field of industrial manufacture, however, will reveal that companies in leading positions care deeply about their products, with attitudes that go far beyond concepts of 'product differentiation' focussed on point-of-sale. Instead their purpose is to satisfy the actual and latent needs of users. More and more frequently, this image is shaped by industrial designers.

Integrating design into the product development process, however, is not achieved simply. The training, the values and professional cultures of such longer-established disciplines as engineering, business administration and marketing differ considerably from those of industrial design. Introducing the latter, or attempting to change its role within a company, requires a managerial structure and policies which clearly recognize the problems involved and consciously works for change. In addition, all the evidence confirms that recognition and strong support at the highest levels of management in any company are required, if the capabilities of designers are to be successfully integrated into an existing structure.

In selecting a subject for the first publication in the Trefoil Design Management series, it was important to select a company which illustrates both the problems and potential of integrating industrial design. In that respect, Philips is an evident example. It is long established, celebrating its centenary in 1991; one of the great giants of the electrical industry among the thirty largest companies in the world. From its origins in the Netherlands, it has become a truly global company, active in over 60 countries and employing some 330,000 people. Annual turnover is currently in the region of US$ 28,000 million and its budget for research and development averages US$ 2,000 million.

Philips was built up by two brothers, one of whom was in charge of technical research, the other commercial strategy. As a result these two aspects have always been accepted as a strength of Philips. The introduction of industrial design came later and for some time it struggled for recognition. A design manager at Philips Corporate Industrial Design, Peter Nagelkerke,

who is the fourth generation of his family to serve the company, jokes that his work would have been much easier had there been a third Philips brother who was an industrial designer. More recently, however, the company has recognized that its enormous capability in research is alone not enough. The results of that research have to be produced in forms which genuinely satisfy consumers needs, in which the use-value is clear, rather than implicit. The contribution design is capable of making to overall strategy is accepted, as is the need for it to be effectively managed.

The book is organized into three parts. Firstly, the origins of the company are set out, with the beginnings of what at first was regarded as the application of art to industry, which later evolved into the modern concept of industrial design. The second part is an account of the current structure of Corporate Industrial Design (CID) in Philips, its role in the company and how it is managed. Finally, a series of case studies illustrate in detail how design is contributing to the process of product development across a broad spectrum of successful types and systems.

When the idea of this book was first discussed with Robert Blaich, Managing Director of CID, I was in the awkward position of asking for his full help and co-operation, whilst stating that, as author, I had to have full right to control the final text. To my great relief, he welcomed an outsider looking at CID and giving a considered view of its achievements and problems. That openness has been a constant feature of my relationship with CID and the extent of my access has been both a privilege and pleasure. In addition to the wholehearted support given to the project by Robert Blaich, his deputy, Frans van der Put, has been an enormous source of help and advice, based on many years at Philips and great wisdom in its ways. I was helped in understanding a crucial period in the development of design at Philips by an interview with Rein Veersema, and Dr. Wisse Dekker, former Chairman of the Board of Management, explained the change of strategy he introduced in the early 1980s. Jan Huyboom, Head of Technical Information at CID was kind enough to loan me considerable quantities of material on the history of design at Philips. My thanks to them and the many other members of CID who spent long hours talking to me and a portable tape-recorder. I would also wish to express my gratitude to Jo Bogers and Yolande Vermeulen of the CID Secretariat who looked after me with a great combination of efficiency and kindness on my visits to Eindhoven. At Ravensbourne College of Design and Communication, my grateful thanks to the Principal, Nicholas Frewing, for his encouragement; to my secretary, Carol Eagles, for her support and good humour; and to the Librarian, John McKay and his staff for their generosity of spirit. The final stages of preparation of the manuscript took place at the Design Management Institute in Boston, Mass., where Earl Powell and his staff provided valuable comment, facilities and support.

Finally, a brief note is necessary on the sources on which the book is based. There is little published on Philips which refers to the evolution of the design function. Two sources were useful on the early history of the company:

A. Heerding's (translated by Derek S. Jordon) *The History of N.V. Philips Gloeilampenfabrieken*, Volume 1, (Cambridge, 1986), and P. J. Bouman, *Growth of an Enterprise: The Life of Anton Philips*, (London, 1956). I am grateful to Professor Robert Hayes of Harvard University for drawing my attention to the autobiography of Frederik Philips, *45 Years with Philips*, (Poole, 1978), which has a useful account of the Philite plant in the 1920s. On more recent policy, a valuable source is *The Dekker Perspective*, a compilation of speeches by the former President of the Philips Board of Management, by D. Overkleeft and L.E. Groosman, (London, 1988). The CID in Eindhoven has much interesting material in the form of documents and publications over many years, but it is incomplete and uncatalogued. This material and conversation with past and present members of Philips have been my main sources, and since it is difficult to reference precisely, I have dispensed with notes and tried to indicate the source in the text.

Contents

Part 4 Conclusion

The development of electrotechnology in the nineteenth century differed markedly from the pragmatic inventions which characterized the early Industrial Revolution, since its progress drew upon an accumulated body of scientific research. For anyone with sufficient technical expertise and entrepreneurial spirit, enormous possibilities opened up if this research could be translated into the manufacture of practical everyday products.

Amongst innovations attracting great attention was the possibility of using electrical current for lighting. A key step was a practicable lamp using a carbon incandescent filament, which both Thomas Edison in the USA and Joseph Swan in Britain developed separately by 1880. To exploit their patent rights the two inventors formed a joint company in 1893, which had a manufacturing monopoly in Britain for ten years, enjoying considerable success.

During this period Gerard Philips (fig. 1) was working in a Glasgow shipyard as a mechanical engineer, after graduating in that subject from Delft University of Technology and studying chemistry at Leiden, and a series of articles on the new carbon filament light in a British technical journal, *The Electrician*, aroused his interest. In 1886 he enrolled on an evening course in 'Electric lighting and transmission of power' at the Glasgow College of Science and Arts. Later he joined a research group at Glasgow University under Sir William Thomson, later Lord Kelvin, one of the great pioneers in the field of electricity and magnetism. Here Gerard

1. Gerard Philips, founder of the company.

Philips' work included testing incandescent lamps. Late in 1887, he obtained employment in the installations department of the Anglo-American Brush Electric Light Company of Loughborough in England and was sent by them to Berlin. There, after meeting Emil Rathenau, the founder of one of Germany's largest electric companies, AEG, he was offered an agency in late 1889, to help negotiate an electricity concession with Amsterdam City Council.

In 1889, four factories already produced electric light bulbs in Holland. As is typical of the early stages of growth of an industry supplying a growing mass-market, these factories were poised between small-scale craft-based production and the introduction of mass-production methods. The future prospects seemed good, since both Amsterdam and Rotterdam planned to develop municipal systems of electric lighting.

Gerard Philips' awareness of this potential led him to consider manufacturing lamps of his own pattern and when his contract with AEG terminated in 1890, his father Frederik provided financial support for a series of experiments to develop a light bulb capable of large-scale manufacture.

Frederik Philips was the sole partner in a banking company and in the firm of Peletier & Philips, which had a tobacco factory and coffee roasting plant at Zaltbommel. The considerable gulf between these traditional commercial and the technical intricacies of factory-based industrial manufacturing did not deter him, however, since his entrepreneurial acumen enabled him to recognize the potential of his son's interest in the new technology.

Early experiments in a make-shift laboratory in Amsterdam seemed promising enough to establish a company, which was founded on May 15th, 1891, with Gerard Philips and his father as the two partners. Premises were obtained in an empty buckskin (fig. 2) factory at Eindh-

3. Anton Philips, the brother of Gerard, and the first commercial director of Philips.

2. The Eindhoven glass factory in a 1920 photograph. The present CID building is on the same site.

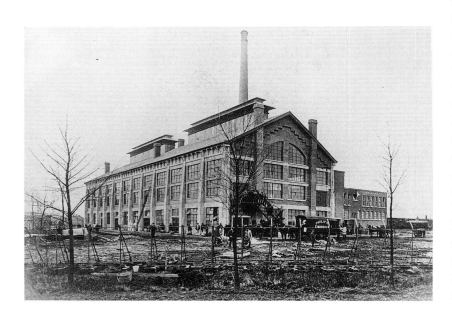

oven, a small town in Brabant in central Holland, with good communicaitons to both Belgium and to Northern and central Germany. Labour was also available there.

The new company faced enormous problems, however, for achievements under laboratory conditions were not so easily transferred to a manufacturing scale. It took a considerable time, firstly for the factory to be equipped, then for staff to be recruited and then trained in their new tasks. This process led in time to production being started, and the business was gradually built up, problems of cost and productivity were resolved, until it became obvious that there was a need for the services of a commercial director. At this time Gerard's younger brother Anton Philips (fig. 3) was in London seeking employment after completing his education at the Public Commercial School in Amsterdam and working there in a stockbroking firm. At his father's request he returned to The Netherlands in January, 1895, to help Gerard by taking over commercial operations for a limited period. The six months to which Anton originally agreed was to become a lifetime and the relationship between the two brothers developed into a remarkable partnership in which each complemented the other. Their co-operation set a pattern for Philips organization, which for many years had two parallel strands of commercial and technical management.

The two brothers realized the company could only be profitable if the scale of production was increased (fig. 4). To reach Gerard's original target of 500 bulbs a day, however, required an effective sales organization and, given the limitations of the Dutch market, opening overseas markets. A start was made in the nearby Rhineland-Westphalia region of Germany, the centre of a huge wave of industrial expansion. By the end of 1895, the target production level was reached and a profit declared on sales of 109,000 bulbs, with production doubling again in the following year.

Anton Philips' successful salesmanship and control of commercial affairs enabled his elder brother to concentrate on research and manufacturing in order to keep pace with growing orders as further overseas markets were opened. Production continued to increase in spectacular fashion, rising from 700,000 units in 1897 to 2,700,000 in 1901, by which time Philips was

4. An early Philips lightbulb.

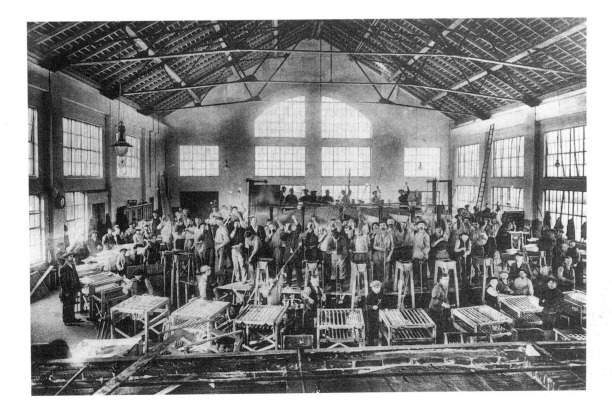

5. Glass-blowers at Eindhoven, 1920.

the third largest producer of light bulbs in Europe. A further index of growth is that in 1893, 25 workers produced 150 lightbulbs per day, whilst in 1903, 500 workers produced 20,000 per day. 1903 also saw the first step away from a purely technical concern in Philips products with the manufacture of a candle-shaped lamp for chandeliers, which turned out to be highly successful. The increase in the scale of activity also required an expansion of technical and commercial staff, of laboratories and offices, as well as production facilities. The light bulb market is one in which market advantage can be achieved by new developments based on advanced research. An example was the metal filament lamp, using tungsten, which first appeared in 1907, and, as it was perfected, took an increasing share of sales.

During the First World War the Netherlands remained neutral. Consequently, Philips in-creased its international market share at the expense of competitors in Britain and Germany, whose production was diverted to the war effort. The war also disrupted supplies of essential materials and components, especially from Germany and Austria-Hungary. As a result, Philips expanded its production facilities, for example, setting-up a glass-making factory in 1916 to compensate for supplies no longer available from Austria (fig. 5). Wartime expansion resul-ted in the number of employees doubling be-tween 1913 and 1919.

In 1922, Gerard Philips retired. He had borne full responsibility for technical develop-ment over many years, but the commercial world and electrical technology were rapidly changing in ways he found unsympathetic. At the age of 48, his brother Anton succeeded him as President of the company, a post he held until 1939.

Inter-war expansion

Under the direction of Anton Philips expansion continued, both in The Netherlands and num-erous subsidiary organizations established in many countries, and Philips evolved into an in-ternational organization, its employees number-ing 18,000 by 1927. The only products were el-ectric light bulbs until 1914, when automobile lamps were first manufactured, followed by pro-jector lamps in 1915. From 1918, however, there began a constant process of diversification (fig. 6). Anton Philips rejected suggestions that the company should enter the field of heavy el-ectrical engineering, steering Philips firmly to-wards consumer goods, for which he had great

6. A selection of Philips projection lamps and radio valves produced between 1918 (foreground) and 1920 to 1927 (back row, left to right).

7. The 1927 Philips radio.

8. Philips radios from the 1930s, and their accompanying advertising material.

enthusiasm. Radio valves, which he believed had a great future, were first produced in 1918. Other radio parts were produced from 1924, loudspeakers from 1926, with radio receivers a year later (fig. 7), and gramophones from 1929. In the 1930s the process accelerated, including such products as microphones, bicycle lamps, sun-ray lamps, X-ray equipment, televisions (1937) and electric shavers (1939). Radio, in particular, had enormous impact (fig. 8). The first Philips set of 1927 was so successful that the workforce at Eindhoven doubled, reaching 20,000 in 1929 to cope with the astonishing demand.

Many new products used bakelite components or housings manufactured from phenolic resin under the brand name of Philite. This

8. Philips radios from the 1930s, and their accompanying advertising material.

was produced in the company's own subsidiary plant established in 1927 (fig. 9). There, Frederik Philips, Anton's son named after his grandfather (fig. 10), was first employed with the company after graduating in mechanical engineering from Delft Technical University and military service organizing production at the Dutch Army Ordnance Factory at Hembrug. In his autobiography he wrote: '. . . it was now vital to have an uninterrupted flow of parts for our increasing production of radio sets, so there was a need for someone who would co-ordinate production and see that delivery deadlines were kept; and this became my responsibility.' The Philite plant thus played an important role in the expansion programme.

In Frederik Philips opinion, the increased scale of production change the status of mechanical engineering within the company. By the 1920s, Philips commitment to research in order to stay at the forefront of innovation and avoid dependence on others patents, required expenditure of up to seven per cent of turn-over. Specialists working in the laboratory therefore had high status, and although mechanical engineers constructed lamp-producing machines, very few were employed in actual production. The introduction of a broad range of products made by assembly line techniques, with supplies coming from various locations, required the skills of mechanical engineers on the shop floor and the co-ordination of production under tight time limits. The Philite plant 'worked round the clock,' wrote Frederik Philips, 'as the hydraulic moulding equipment and other expensive tools had to earn their keep, and continuous production was needed to reduce waiting times and meet delivery dates.'

In fact, higher levels of skill were needed throughout the company and on the initiative of

Anton Philips, the Trades School at Eindhoven (fig. 11) began courses to train skilled industrial craftsmen, particularly machine tool makers. Further training as in draughtsmanship was also possible. Frederik Philips wrote: 'A great many of the trainees rose far above being skilled workers. Some became designers, others became departmental chiefs, others continued their technical education, and a few became engineers. One became a university professor. . . . But from our point of view, the finest aspect of the venture was that the level of craftsmanship in our own factories improved considerably.'

9. The Philite plant, established in 1927.

10. Frederik Philips, the son of Anton Philips, seen with Robert Blaich in a photograph taken in 1985.

11. The Trades School at Eindhoven.

The Origins of Design at Philips

The diversification into consumer goods required as a further corollary an increase in advertising to reach the mass-market necessary to sustain mass-production. This was initially the responsibility of the 'Advertising Section' which in 1928 became the 'Propaganda Section', the usual term at that time for publicity, advertising and promotion. No direct evidence exists of any employment of applied artists or what would later be called industrial designers in the company prior to 1925.

In January of that year, however, Louis Kalff (fig. 12), an architect trained at the Technical University at Delft, joined the Advertising Section with responsibility for the artistic aspects of advertising, products and some architecture. In an interview in 1950, Kalff said the post resulted from his contacting Anton Philips with suggestions for improving company publicity.

12. Louis Kalff.

13. The stars and waves design, by Kalff, on an early radio.

PHILIPS

At first he worked on lamp and radio valve packaging and in 1926 produced a design which included the stars and waves that later evolved into the company emblem, the first consistent element of Philips visual identity to be established (fig. 13).

In December, 1928, an internal company document announced the establishment of a Propaganda Centre to combine all services relating to advertising or propaganda. It consisted of four independent departments: PC1, for Commercial Propaganda; PC2, Literary Propaganda (including the Press Office); PC3, Technical Propaganda, and PC4, Artistic Propaganda (led by Louis Kalff). The Centre was intended to coordinate campaigns based on sales programmes drafted by the commercial department, acting as intermediary between the latter and its four constituent departments. It was emphasized that programmes should take into account taste differences existing in Latin, Anglo-Saxon, German and South American markets, with Eindhoven forming 'a relationship with a prominent advertising agency having connections with well known artists versed in the four areas' varying tastes. The specific tasks of the Artistic Propaganda Section were firstly the design of posters, showcards, series advertisements, and the illustration of brochures, secondly, co-operation on exhibitions, thirdly co-operation on display services, fourthly, the dissemination of successful designs received from branches amongst all other branches in co-operation with the Commercial Department. They were also to supply all branches (wherever possible) with skilled artistic designs appropriate to their country, to supervise the purchase of advertising materials and in general have the aesthetic care of Philips products.

In 1929, Louis Kalff's growing interest in lighting technique led to the establishment of a Lighting Advisory Bureau (Lichtadvies Bureau) within the company. Its early work included advice on lighting to several Dutch towns and to major international exhibitions at Barcelona (1929), Antwerp (1930, where the idea of indirect lighting was introduced), Brussels (1935) and Paris (1938) (fig. 14).

In 1932, the Light Advisory Group (LIBU) and the Artistic Propaganda Section (ARTO) were formally grouped together under the direction of Kalff. Their relative roles were that LIBU undertook major projects across the world, such as exhibitions, whilst ARTO was responsible for product and packaging design. Whether Kalff was himself responsible for the design of all Philips first consumer products, the radios of 1927 onwards, is not clear and designs may even have been supplied from outside the company. The records are scant and many early accounts erroneously attribute the whole of Philips design in this period to him. The number of people who worked with Kalff is also unclear; there were apparently several interior designers and one member of his staff who not only worked for Philips, but also as a free-lance designer for outside commissions. One certain fact is that the loudspeaker of the first 1927 radio was chosen from several possible shapes by Anton Philips himself, the shape being considered by him to be most suitable for Dutch mantelpieces.

Nevertheless, Kalff's role in the development of design not only in the company, but in the Netherlands, was considerable. According to Frans van der Put, he was heavily influenced in

LES PAVILLONS PHILIPS A L'EXPOSITION DE BRUXELLES 1935
DE PHILIPS PAVILJOENS OP DE TENTOONSTELLING VAN BRUSSEL 1935   Ing. L C KALFF
Arch. H v d PAUWERT

his views by the example of the German Werkbund, and he was a founder, member and first chairman of the K.I.O., the Dutch designers association. He was employed by Philips in different capacities for thirty-five years with wide-ranging influence on visual forms emanating from the company, being consulted for a considered opinion on all aesthetic questions. His role as unofficial advisor to Anton Philips on his personal artistic collection, which gave him continual informal access to the head of the company, was undoubtedly important in this respect.

Other influences in the company, however,

14. The Philips stands at the Paris and Brussels exhibitions.

such as the technical designers and sales section, also had considerable capacity to affect product forms. It seems likely that decisions on new models were based on technical innovations or marketing assessments, with considerations of form following from these. The lack of detailed evidence, apart from anecdote, however, makes it difficult to estimate exactly what was decisive in particular cases.

Kalff's work evidently answered a need, however, for through the 1930s, the number of staff engaged on various design functions in the company increased. Until 1933, Kalff had alone been responsible for packaging, but in that year had been joined by an Austrian named Bieber. By January, 1939, LIBU had five light advisors, five lighting designers, several illustrators and a packaging design group. Other designers, some from other countries such as Czechoslovakia, France and Denmark, were employed on short term assignments.

Depression and War

By 1930, no company could ignore the impact of the Great Depression, which began to increasingly affect Philips. Between 1931-33 the workforce declined from 28,000 to 16,000 due to lay-offs resulting from declining sales and financial losses. Anton Philips managed the company in a paternalistic manner, a term of disapproval today, but which in the context of his time meant concern for the welfare of his workforce, and the many difficult decisions taken made this a painful time. On one aspect, however, Philips did not cut back, and that was Research and Development, regarded as the lifeblood of the future.

Steering the company through the Depression

was, however, a heavy burden for Anton Philips and the strain undoubtedly contributed to an illness requiring a long convalescence in 1936. Consequently, the management of the company had to be reorganized. Whilst Anton remained President, control of day-to-day operations was handed to his son-in-law, Frans Otten (fig. 15), with the title of Managing Director. Responsibility for specific functions was formally given to three senior colleagues, including Frederik Philips, Anton's son, who joined the Board of Directors. The scale of activity had simply become too great for one man to handle and acceptance of the principle of multiple authority in management was a necessary change.

Despite problems and uncertainties, the range of products manufactured by Philips in this period continued to expand. Frederik Philips wrote: 'The regular flow of new products played a predominant part in the expansion of Philips, both before and after the war. Indeed, half of our turn-over has usually consisted of products which we were not manufacturing, or which had not even been thought of, ten years before.' Experiments in the 1930s included fields such as television (fig. 16) (Philips sets were on sale in Britain in 1937), nuclear physics, welding techniques, X-rays and magnetics. All these found their way into product development of various kinds. On an everyday level, however, the most significant introduction was probably the Philishave dry-shaver, which has become an enduring line, continuously refined (fig. 17).

15. Frans Otten, managing director of Philips in 1936, later President.

The political tensions of the late 1930s in Europe led Philips to take precautionary measures, such as moving some research facilities to Britain and taking legal measures preventing Philips property abroad being declared enemy property should the Netherlands be occupied. No amount of foresight, however, could soften the pain of actuality after the country was overrun in May, 1940, and the company was hard-hit by the occupation. Many top staff escaped to help run subsidiaries in Britain and the USA and elsewhere, but Frederick Philips stayed to try and keep the Dutch company intact and protect the interests of the workforce. He was subjected to German administrators appointed to oversee the company and under constant investigation. Production was hampered by lost markets, and workers who formerly took pride in quality work, now did everything possible to conceal slackness and unreliability as a form of resistance. Some were shot during demonstrations. Frederick Philips and his wife both suffered imprisonment, as did other employees, and large numbers were deported as forced labour to Germany. Many did not survive. Despite the Eindhoven Factories being known to the Dutch as the 'British fortress' it was twice bombed by the Royal Air Force, inevitably with loss of life and considerable damage (fig. 18).

16. A large screen television set from 1938, and other sets from the 1939 range.

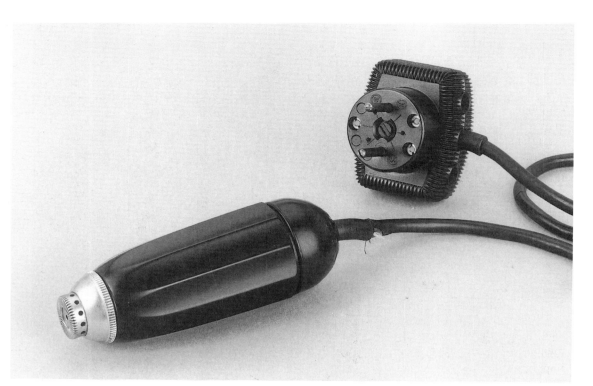

17. The first Philips dry shaver.

18. Photograph of an air raid on Philips, from one of the attacking aircraft.

Post-war reconstruction

After the war an enormous task of reconstruction awaited on every level and it took time before any semblance of normality could be re-established (fig. 19). At first, the company reverted to the pre-war organizational structure established in 1936, with a four-man Board of Directors. The daunting scale of problems, however, meant that the management tasks requiring solution were beyond the capabilities of four people. Frans Otten, therefore, became **President** and Frederik Philips **Vice-President**, with the Board of Directors turned into a Board of Management, with five members. In 1957, the Board was further enlarged to cope with further growth.

Perhaps the most profoundly important decision of the 1946 re-organization was a fundamental re-structuring of the company, with two important consequences. Firstly, the manufacturing side was divided into a number of product divisions, which under commercial and technical directors, were responsible for policy world-wide. New divisions were later established as necessary to meet changing technical or market conditions. Secondly, the national organizations (NOs), responsible for local manufacturing and marketing, were organized into a federated structure under overall control of the enlarged Board of Management in Eindhoven.

The Product Divisions were located in the Netherlands, with the later exception of Major Domestic Appliances which in 1974 was established in Italy. They were responsible for world-wide product policy, both technically and commercially. The concept was that quality of products and systems could be ensured by them building in continuity from the development and design stage, through production, to after-sales service.

The National Organizations operated within the laws and regulations of their own country and ranged from purely marketing organizations to complex industrial enterprises controlling product development, design and production for the local market. Although having considerable autonomy, they were intended to consult and co-operate with the Product Divisions.

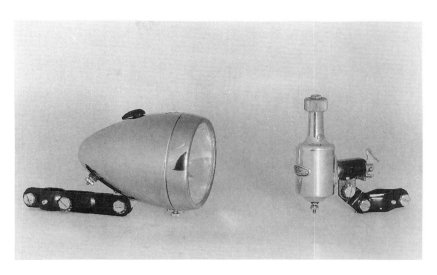

By 1950 the process of recovery was turning into a new phase of expansion. The extensive research facilities of the company again proved a major strength and were at the heart of numerous developments. Perhaps the great strength of Philips research has been a capacity to follow independent lines of investigation, rather than being tied to existing market-determined concepts. The result has been continuous technical innovation and a flow of new products coming on line (fig. 20). As a consequence, development, design and production facilities both in The Netherlands and abroad rapidly grew. A further

19. A bicycle lamp produced by Philips immediately after the war, a stop gap product while full facilities were being rebuilt.

20a. Post-war radio set.

growth factor was a series of acquisitions of other companies across the world, expanding both production capacity and the range of products.

The changes in the product-range and in the nature of markets, including that for labour, led to Philips emerging by the 1960s as a genuinely international company. In 1965, of the total of 252,000 employees, only 87,000 were located in The Netherlands.

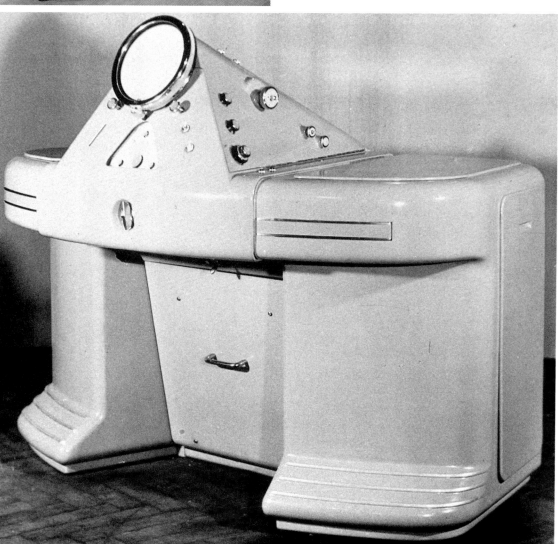

20b. Two examples of Post-War medical equipment.

Design in the Post-war Period

This changing pattern in the company as a whole was also reflected in the organization of the design function. In 1946 Louis Kalff was appointed a director of the Product Division Light, with responsibility for the design function, still divided into LIBU and ARTO. He was a member of the product division management team reporting to its chairman. ARTO, however, although part of Product Division Lighting, also worked for other divisions. Detailed information on the structure and procedures of the organization of design is again lacking, but apparently both groups were still relatively small. In the early 1950s the product group had four members who were draughtsmen, recruited from the factory because of their drawing ability. Beyond its responsibility to Kalff who supervised and directed their work, the group had no formal organization. Models and drawings were still submitted to the Commercial Departments who could change them at will, without consultation. Little evidence also exists regarding the use of outside consultants, though in 1948, Raymond Loewy was responsible for the Philishave electric razor of that year (fig. 21).

In 1953, however, the Artistic Propaganda Department was split, with Kalff continuing to head the light section LIBU, and a radio section being delegated to work within the Product Division Apparatus, which manufactured such products as radios, televisions, record-players, shavers and coffee-mills. The crucial position of these products in company sales led to a demand for a group to service their needs specifically. Its head, who still reported to Kalff, was Rein Veersema (fig. 22), an architect trained at the Technical University, Delft, who began work in the Light Division in 1950.

The two men came from wholly different generations. Veersema represented the newly-emerging discipline of industrial design. He understood mass-production and its technical aspects, accepting that in a large commercial organization design should be anonymous, a team effort dependent on co-operation with other disciplines. This challenged Kalff's long-

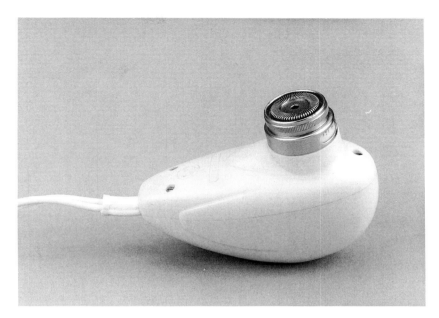

established belief in applying art to industry and the attitude he reputedly represented of 'If I can draw it, they can make it!' The existence of two groups responsible for design, reflecting such different standpoints, created many difficulties and tensions. However, the section under Veersema rapidly grew in importance and in 1954 it became independent of Kalff.

21. The 1948 electric razor, designed by Raymond Loewy.

22. Rein Veersema.

The Apparatus Design Group

A company regulatory document dated 31 August, 1954, published by the Product Division, Apparatus, contained the outcome of discussions with Louis Kalff, which established a new design group, titled 'Apparaten Vormgeving' (AV) or 'Apparatus Design'. It was placed under the jurisdiction of Technical Director Bouman of the Apparatus Division, although the Commercial Manager, Mr. Leeuwin, was responsible for the appearance of products. The role of AV was in the first instance to design the appearance of products so as to, on one hand, extend sales possibilities and 'to strive for original forms and/or ways of decoration'; on the other hand to comply with demands for 'good taste, technique, construction, and cost price limits,' taking into account the need 'to adapt to fashion tastes in the different sales areas, as indicated by the commercial department.' To do this, the AV group was required to undertake a research function into possible appearances, new materials and working methods and to make models of emerging ideas, thus enabling AV 'to be well-prepared and not to have deliver hurriedly made, ill-considered designs due to the pressures of commercial or factory planning.' AV's further brief was to develop discussion and improvement of designs from overseas sources by 'international co-operation with and service to those authorities within the foreign Philips organizations in charge of design, and those who do not possess a design group', and finally 'to advise on design and manufacturing problems as well as developments on new techniques as far as these influence the appearance.'

The document concluded: 'To be able to achieve quick responses, necessary for keeping to development planning times, regular consultations during the various design stages are a must. Moreover it is very important to research valuable new ideas regardless of their origin.' The document marked a new emphasis on the development of products rather than on advertising and packaging and in this respect it can be seen, in principle at least, as the embryo of what was later to emerge as the modern industrial design function at Philips, though there was no sudden, dramatic change of direction.

The difficulties of reconciling the polished phrases of policy documents on the role of design with the reality of practice became evident, however, after AV was established. Decisions on products to be manufactured and procedures to be undertaken, were taken by the product Committee (PROCO) of the Product Division Apparatus. It became clear, though, that a considerable gulf existed between the decisions of PROCO and the often long-established attitudes of personnel dispersed in various sections who executed the work. To achieve consistency of decision-making and practice, Article Teams were established, with representatives of engineering, marketing and design, responsible for each major product or product group, thus giving designers some possibility of participating in decision-making. However, their role was still a subsidiary one, which could be, and frequently was, overruled by commercial managers. An anecdote from a designer at that time is illustrative. When preparing models for radio housings, he and a colleague decided to experiment with aluminium trim instead of the gold colour habitually used. When presented to the commercial director, he not only vehemently rejected the idea, but after the meeting furiously assaulted the model housing with a screwdriver and replaced the silver coloured trim with the conventional gold. The irrational rejection of what departed from accepted norms was hardly an incentive for innovative thinking and, indeed, many people in the organization still regarded the function of design as little more than the superficial styling of what had already been determined elsewhere.

Yet despite such problems, there was also progress, and before long, other product divisions began to request AV to undertake work. Its increase in staffing from 8 in late 1956 to 17 in 1960 was indicative of this growth, which was mainly by taking young designers from the Akademie voor Industriële Vormgeving in Eindhoven, where evening courses in industrial design commenced in 1950. Veersema took young, talented craftsmen from the factory and sent them on this course to develop the new attitudes he felt was required in design. 'Most of the people to begin with', he recalled, 'were only educated in the public schools, but were top craftsmen. I was always interested in these sort of people because they knew what quality was.' Some major figures of Philips design in subsequent years, such as Frans van der Put, Piet van Leeuwarden, Harry Heinemans and Ruud Zijlstra, were all graduates of the first group to complete this course, joining Philips between 1953 and 1955. Joop van Osnabrugge, another recruit, was, however, a graduate of a shorter three year course started slightly later in the design school at The Hague.

A consequence of this expansion of work by AV was that it began to compete with LIBU for commissions. An added complication was that in 1958, due to the rapid expansion of product ranges, the Product Division Apparatus was divided into two new divisions, Small Domestic Appliances (SDA) and Radio, Gramophone and Television (RGT). Veersema's group remained within the latter, but continued to service the needs of both. Indeed, when SDA established a new plant at Drachten in the north of The Netherlands, two designers were detached to provide design expertise on site.

The situation was therefore rapidly becoming confused. A clear demand for design services was emerging from Product Divisions but was being satisfied in an ad hoc manner, since Kalff's personal style of leadership did not include a management policy or structure that allowed new developments to evolve within an overall policy or organization.

The Industrial Design Bureau

Demand for their design services might be increasing, but the designers felt their contribution could not be really effective without a clearer recognition of their role, which was difficult to establish whilst still subordinate to commercial management. Veersema, who was an idealist with a clear concept of what the role of design should be, did not have a good relationship with managers who regarded AV as a puppet organization which should dance to their tune. He accepted the discipline of working for a large company, but, as he subsequently put it, 'for quality reasons not commercial reasons.' He therefore began a campaign to persuade the Board of Management of the importance of industrial design and the need for it to be established as a central function with a corporate task. He believed an independent organization with influence on product policy decisions was the only way to control design quality. Problems already existed with design groups in many national organizations independently producing designs for so-called 'local-for-local' products, of variable quality. If commercially successful, however, these products frequently slipped over

boundaries to become generally available, sometimes even competing with centrally designed products (fig. 23).

These efforts proved successful when the Concern Bureau Vormgeving (Industrial Design Bureau – the word Concern meaning Corporation or Company in Dutch) was established as a

23a. One of a selection of Philips products from 1961 to 1965.

result of a Board of Management decision in 1960. The department consisted of members of

23b. A selection of Philips products from 1961 to 1965.

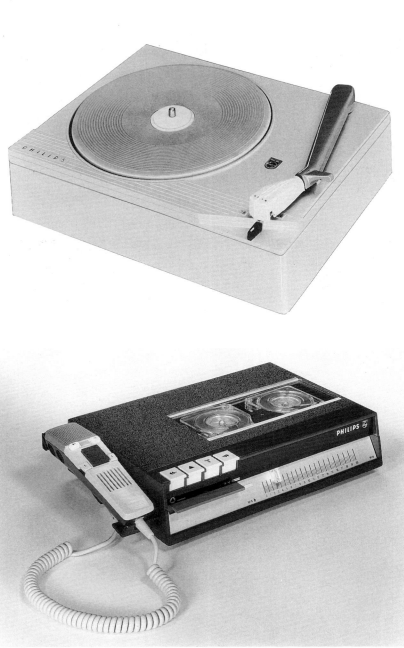

design within the concern as a whole, preventing different divisions and particularly national organizations from setting up separate design units.

Although the new status of designers helped in their day-to-day activities, it did not, of course, automatically solve all their problems. Veersema therefore set out to develop new competences in such areas as ergonomics and costing so designers could reinforce their case with the product divisions. 'They were not accustomed to this', he recalls, 'they thought I was the chap who makes a nice form.' (fig. 24)

In a press release of the following year, 1961, Rein Veersema set out his idea of industrial design as the unification of 'both aesthetic and scientific refinement'. His concept of design was of a mode of thought rather than specific visual techniques. Collaboration between divisions was therefore cited by him as evidence that 'Design' was at work before the technical development process was completed and the first sketches were produced. The circumstances under which a product would be applied, that is user requirements, including ergonomics, required consideration during the phase of technical development and in addition, Veersema cited such factors as quality levels, price, packaging, materials and economic aspects which all helped determine the ultimate form and colour.

One of the most important aspects of the work of the Design Bureau was defined by Veersema as the creation of an affinity in the shaping of products, 'the creation of a 'family feature', identifying Philips as the manufacturer at first glance.' A start had been made, he said, on professional products, such as cinema apparatus, but since household appliances had such different functions they presented more difficulties. 'It is in this way,' he said, 'that propaganda value is turned to commercial account, since constant repetition of the same features appears to be an expression of the fact that the quality is known to be good. . . . It has been shown that the instant the public sees the form and colour of a product is the instant when belief in its quality is born. It is therefore impor-

24. Photography for the 1956 Mignon record player.

tant that uniformity in design should be striven for as a prop to the 'recognition value'.'

Veersema also expressed his views on frequent changes in the form of products, arguing that departing from a familiar design signified the previous product was inadequate. 'Important elements of previous programmes can be continued in the new', he said. 'There is abundant room for an evolutionary movement towards ever new and more progressive conceptions and for a continuation of the process of rapid adaptation to new standards.' Uniformity did not mean every product had to look alike, neither did it imply sterility in design. 'Constant technical improvement and high quality will always lead to an exterior correct down to the last detail and exuding both vitality and modernity', he concluded.

The contribution of Rein Veersema to establishing design as a discipline at Philips was substantial. He successfully battled to have design recognised as a corporate function and he constantly sought to upgrade the overall quality

of staff in the Bureau Vormgeving and the efficacy of working procedures. He introduced the idea of structuring the product development process by the use of Article Teams comprising the main contributory disciplines of production, marketing and industrial design. Inevitably, there was a high degree of improvisation involved in setting up and operating the new Bureau, but Frans van der Put recalls him working in a democratic manner, involving everyone in the development of new ideas and procedures. Yet he was also an idealist, impatient to build up the Bureau and realize its potential as he saw it.

In 1964 , he submitted a document to the Board of Management, setting out his ideas for future policy and procedures regarding design within Philips, encapsulated in thirteen main points, as follows:
'1. The Concern should make a clear statement at the highest level on the policy with respect to design.

2. A general form of organization for design in the company is necessary.

3. A more critical attitude towards standards of industrial products in the company is required.

4. A common policy on the functional level of industrial designers is necessary if an effective working situation is to be created.

5. In those countries where product development is at a level requiring industrial design to be based there, designers should be appointed.

6. Where this is not the case, the Concern Bureau Vormgeving should be responsible.

7. The designers must be integrated into the technical organization in order to guarantee an effective and continuing relationship with the development teams.

8. In addition, in the Concern Bureau Vormgeving as well as the national organizations, designers must be incorporated in the article teams.

9. In countries where designers are working autonomously, they should operate as part of the respective article groups and should not be regarded as an independent operator.

10. Concern products which can be manufactured in international product centres should be the responsibility of Product Division management and the local designer should be regarded as a delegate of the Concern Bureau Vormgeving.

11. Only when the level of industrial design in all countries is comparable, will it be possible to call an international design meeting which can report to product committees.

12. It is not important who designs, what is designed, or where in the Philips organization design takes place, as long as it is on the basis of a common positive and qualitative policy and rules.

13. A good industrial design policy will never be directed towards the prestige of the industrial designer but will always represent and result in the prestige of Philips products.'

Veersema's list represented a concept of design in many respects ahead of its time, particularly his understanding of it as an integral, cooperative activity with other specialisms, and the need for common standards throughout the company. To achieve his ends required pat-

25. Frans van der Put.

ience and political skills. However, it was not in his nature to compromise and realizing his ideas were not going to be quickly implemented, he decided to resign.

After Veersema's departure in 1965, Frans van der Put (fig. 25), who had been his deputy since 1960, took over as interim head, a post he held for two years. His initial concern was to stabilize the situation after the departure of Veersema, since in some quarters in the company, the role of design was being placed in question. Van der Put shared Veersema's idealism, believing that design should prove itself by its works, in a spirit of wanting to do things better, of making products that contributed to an improvement in the world. He was also astute enough to recognize, however, that the design function should avoid unnecessary controversy and be organized in a way that practically demonstrated its value. In this quiet aim, he was wholly successful.

However, in considering a permanent successor as head of design, the Board of Management determined to look outside the company for a figure of international repute to give the design function a new impetus in line with the growing international markets of Philips. This was a new departure in management appointments but subsequently became part of a general policy of continuity on the second level and renewal at the top. Frans van der Put saw it as a tribute to the growing professionalism of design

and its position in the company, for which he and Veersema had long worked.

Scandinavian design was enjoying a considerable vogue world-wide at this time and seemed to offer a suitable model for emulation. After a process of search and interview, Knut Yran from Norway was appointed as the new director of design in 1966.

Concern Industrial Design Centre

A poet and painter as well as designer, Knut Yran (fig. 26) had an international reputation through his free-lance work. He was a large man, both physically and in personality, a volatile enthusiast who generated strong emotions and who threw himself into his new job with great energy. Design, he stressed, was 'a technical profession with a marketing function' and a designer 'must realize the concern's intentions before he realizes those of his own'. Soon after his arrival he changed the name of the design organization from Concern Bureau Vormgeving to Concern Industrial Design Centre (CIDC), a title he thought would reflect an international rather than a predominantly Dutch emphasis. His efforts initially concentrated on reorganization and devising new procedures.

By 1969 Yran had completed an organizational structure for CIDC, which in principle was to last throughout his directorship.

26. Knut Yran.

Concern Industrial Design Centre Operational Scheme 1969

A booklet outlining the structure and operation of CIDC published internally in 1970, made it clear that responsibility in this pattern rested ultimately with the Director, who determined the general policy 'assisted and advised by the Design Staff (DESTA)'. It was a hierarchical system (fig. 27). 'Project briefs', ideas or request for a project were discussed at DESTA meetings and translated into a specific 'design brief'. Co-ordinators on DESTA then delegated group leaders in charge of design teams to complete a given project. The group leader was responsible for maintaining contact with the technical and commercial staff involved in the project. In reverse, 'Designers report their problems, requirements, needs and so forth – as well as their working intentions – to their group leaders, who in turn will report to DESTA . . . ' Weekly meetings of DESTA then monitored the progress of projects.

Another change in organizational structure under Knut Yran was a postscript to the different perceptions of Louis Kalff and Rein Veersema. These were finally resolved in 1973,

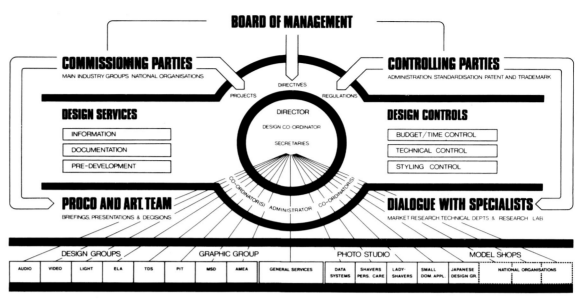

27. CIDC operations
scheme.

when the final step in integrating all Philips design activities under a single management was completed, with the design group of the Product Division Light, the remnant of the group originally established by Kalff, being integrated into CIDC.

The first four years of Yran's directorship brought rapid growth in the number of staff employed by CIDC. The new organization and the increasing range of competences represented in its ranks helped boost the confidence and enabled a number of new initiatives to emerge. For

28. Philips radio
products, 1970, showing
the 'family' approach.

example, in the Audio division there was a move in the late 1960s to think in terms of product range with an overall family resemblance, rather than individual products (fig. 28). However, the organizational plan for CIDC specified a management process with the design group, but did not identify a pattern of linkage to other functions in the company, and there were still frequent difficulties in relationships with the Product Divisions. Their managers

often continued to regard design as a late, superficial addition to the process of product development and could still impose ideas upon product design, for example, insisting on wood instead of metal for housings. Proselytizing the virtues of design, no matter with how much conviction, was clearly not enough to achieve the fundamental change of attitude needed in this respect.

The Design Track

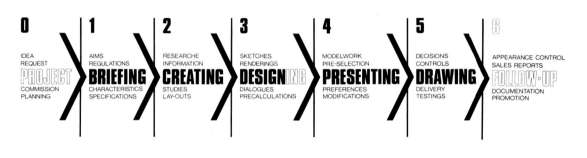

0	1	2	3	4	5	6
IDEA REQUEST	AIMS REGULATIONS	RESEARCHE INFORMATION	SKETCHES RENDERINGS	MODELWORK PRE-SELECTION	DECISIONS CONTROLS	APPEARANCE CONTROL SALES REPORTS
PROJECT	BRIEFING	CREATING	DESIGNING	PRESENTING	DRAWING	FOLLOW-UP
COMMISSION PLANNING	CHARACTERISTICS SPECIFICATIONS	STUDIES LAY-OUTS	DIALOGUES PRECALCULATIONS	PREFERENCES MODIFICATIONS	DELIVERY TESTINGS	DOCUMENTATION PROMOTION

29. The Design Track expressed in visual form.

Another early measure by Yran was to establish control over the designers' mode of working with a method of systematic planning, which was a widespread concern in the design world of the late 1960s. This focussed on a concept called the 'Design Track' which he established as part of CIDC's rules (fig. 29). 'As design is more problem-solving than artistry,' he wrote, 'the definition of the design problem is half of the job! I therefore made a design track realizing the essential importance of careful investigation, the collection of all relevant facts before you start. Half of the story of successful industrial design is to be found in the briefing stages.' It was intended to safeguard efficiency and teamwork yet leaving room for the designer's 'main task of problem solving and creativity.'

Though subsequently refined in detail, the Design Track remained unaltered in basic principle and was clearly central to Yran's concept of his role as Director. 'The more proficient the runner,' he wrote, 'the further he will be from his goal if he runs in the wrong direction! The main task of design management must be to assist in collating the relevant information pos-

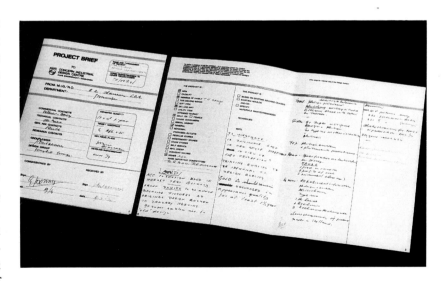

sessed by all the parties concerned in a project brief. To a surprising extent the creative process is in formulating the problem.' The introduction of a formal written brief for any project was an important move. Previously there had been verbal briefings, but without adequate documentation of decisions it subsequently became easy for varying interpretations to be put forward.

30. The Project Brief, used to monitor design progress.

A review of the Design Track in 1972 again emphasized the brief which was now formalized as a four-page document on which as much initial information as possible was plotted with a statement of aims to be achieved (fig. 30). It included a schedule for different phases of the project, with an estimate of costs. The function of time-sheet, together with noted expenses, enabled the cost of each project to be traced immediately. The document was also used to log subsequent alterations to instructions, schedules or budget decisions. A copy of the time-table was posted in the room where the weekly DESTA meetings took place, indicating progress through the various phases. Designers were required to have a copy available in pockets specifically provided for the purpose on the project board by their work station, and group leaders also had to keep a copy. It was therefore a document of central importance in controlling the affairs of CIDC, not only of de-

sign projects, but also of other functions, such as administration, co-ordination, and supervision.

'Designing never starts with designing' wrote Yran, introducing the second phase of the design Track, titled 'Investigation'. This consisted of preparing relevant information from the commissioning group and CIDC files. It covered such factors as product concept, technical specifications, available materials and processes, ergonomics, safety and servicing recommendations, and aesthetic trends. Information on relevant competitive products on the market was also included.

With briefing completed, work could begin on the next stage of 'designing'. Whilst acknowledging the need for dialogue and teamwork, Yran stressed the creative process was always an individual contribution, capable of development through many means and media. Design differed from art in focussing on what the pro-

31. A DESTA meeting. The switches in front of Knut Yran control the lighting and remote TV camera used to inspect the models placed on the central turntable.

duct would communicate rather than self-expression. 'The design work', he wrote, using a favourite metaphor, 'is nothing but an organization of bits and pieces of information tiles into a mosaic – a mosaic being always more than the sum of its parts.'

At DESTA meetings, two control points were emphasized (fig. 31). The first, in the phase of 'Pre-selection', assessed initial ideas in the form of sketches, renderings, clay studies or three-dimensional models, giving reactions and suggesting modifications, and taking decisions on whether proposals could be progressed further. The second control point was the presentation of final models, when designs were released for approval from the commissioner, the Product Division, for production.

A major problem however, lay in the sheer weight of projects DESTA had to process, at a rate of some 800 each year. With inadequate time for detailed analysis in every case, inevitably subjective criteria played a role in the decision making process.

A New House Style

The most significant project of Yran's early years, was his involvement in the definition of a new House Style for Philips, based on a manual comprising mandatory standards for all aspects of visual design within the company. Until his arrival, the graphic aspects of projects were dealt with by the designer responsible. The establishment of a specialist graphic design section within CIDC provided necessary expertise, but a more fundamental problem was that as the company had grown in size, complexity and geographical spread, variations in advertising, exhibitions and publications had developed. There was an obvious need for measures to coordinate the company's visual image and establish greater consistency of presentation. A study group was therefore established, in which Knut Yran played a leading role, to carry out a comprehensive image study as a basis for drafting a House Style Manual (fig. 32). Three major arguments were advanced for the manual: it would lead to economies in work and decision time, it would safeguard the legal position of Philips house marks, and it would be a crucial element in image building. On the latter Yran wrote: 'Let's remember: people don't read, they recognize! People don't buy products, but confidence, confidence is based on recognition, recognition on repetition.' The aim was consistent adherence to defined visual standards throughout the world to enable 'the mosaic to be more than the sum of its parts.' The House Style Manual was officially launched on the 1st January 1973 and revised in 1977. It was undoubtedly successful in protecting the Philips house marks, but the problems of effectively controlling its application throughout the Philips empire restricted its effect in other respects.

32. The House Style Manual first published in 1973 and revised in 1977.

Communication and Updating

33. Typical spread from Design Signals, the CIDC newsletter.

The dissemination of information on current developments in design theory and practice and in technology was also a feature of Yran's policy. The CIDC in-house journal was relaunched under the title Design Signals and besides company news, also included short articles on such themes as ergonomics and computer designing, then in its infancy (fig. 33). Information letters and 'slide circles' were other means used to keep staff informed.

Yran was also capable of recognizing that new ideas and materials could result in very different approaches to the kinds of form which emerged from CIDC. In 1969 he wrote: 'Rectangular and other geometrically simple forms, really leaves it to be questioned whether designers have recognized in full the wonderful possibilities of for instance plastic materials, so willingly waiting to be sculpted in more humanized forms, etched less aggressively and more inviting the product into the use in our hands.' Yet there is little evidence that such thoughts were translated into concrete ideas or procedures which resulted in changes to the forms actually produced. In several respects there was a gulf between Yran's capacity for significant insight and ideas and his ability to realize them through conscious managerial policy and procedures in an institutional context.

The demands of the National Organizations for design expertise for 'local for local' products also presented continuing problems. In the late 1960s design staff were locally appointed for the industrial design function throughout Philips worldwide, for example in such countries as India and Mexico, with the advice of senior staff from CIDC. By such means Philips made a contribution to the development of industrial design in many countries. However, creating a sense of identity amongst designers scattered across numerous locations was problematic. Secondment of individuals to Eindhoven was possible, but a major initiative to bring all Philips designers together was a series of seminars. Organized biannually, they alternated between Eindhoven and an overseas location, with presentations by distinguished visitors as well as members of the company's various divisions. The first in 1968 brought together some 105 Philips designers from all over the world to hear such luminaries as Raymond Loewy and Henri Henrion, though the emphasis was evidently as much social as professional, intended to create a sense of belonging to what Yran referred to as the 'Philips design family'. Such gatherings were useful on many levels, though they failed to prevent the problem of local designs diverging from, or even competing with, CIDC products and standards.

In another initiative soon after his arrival, Yran established a small Predevelopment Group with CIDC to explore speculative futuristic possibilities, emphasizing that although practical considerations were crucial, 'Nevertheless, it is necessary to dream.' An early project in the late 1960s, which he initiated, was the Teacher-aiding Electronic Learning Link (T. E. L. L.) project as a contribution to International Education Year, 1970. Its aim was to demonstrate how electronic media could lead to more effective teaching and learning (fig. 34). Design for an integrated electronic console for each pupil in a class were drawn and modelled, but more than the hardware, the project illustrated Yran's idealism regarding the way design could shape the future. 'The multiplication of tape and the computer's capabilities forces us to re-evaluate present positions and adopt new policies. This is the challenge to responsible authorities, this is the challenge to the teaching profession unnecessarily wasting its capacity on administering routines which could be electronically assisted – but first of all it is also a challenge to the graphic designer and visual communicator in tomorrow's world.' Above all the

system was intended to benefit students: '. . . first and foremost, the system is designed to fill a new and important function in today's school: to give the pupils enquiring minds, and to teach them how to sift and acquire knowledge. They will be able to learn how to learn.' It was the use of knowledge that was emphasized: 'People knowing the theory of music but not able to move to its rhythms; a world that is literate but unmoved by poetry, would mean battles won but a war lost.' The idealism behind the project was entirely sympathetic, and a presentation of it by Yran to an international conference in 1970 was memorable. With hindsight, however, it was a visionary, high cost concept that showed little understanding of contemporary educational economics. In 1973, other projects included a video-disc player, a future kitchen, an inner-city car and a new hair-drier concept, not all of which were produced at the time (fig. 35). However, Yran was clear in his opinion of the usefulness of such projects. 'Utopia', he wrote, 'has been too handy a household name for brushing

34. The T.E.L.L. system in model form: it was never commercially developed.

35. Other 1973 projects included the Town Car and a Video Disc Player.

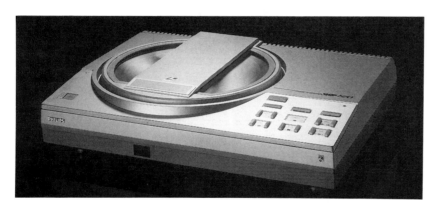

off annoying observations. But the archaeology of dreams will soon show that today's realities build on many of the utopian visions unearthed in the topsoil of the centuries.'

An important channel of communication which Yran effectively used was his occasional reports to the Board of Management. By the early 1970s, the impact of Japanese competition was becoming evident and was the subject of a report, prepared within CIDC, which Yran presented to the Board in March 1973. The 28 page document had a bare summary on its cover:

'A comparative appearance-survey on the differences in material choice and use, the technical-finish quality and the production quality of some Japanese versus Philips portable radios and radio recorders.

This results in a strong warning about Japanese competition in the following respects:
— Obviously Japanese design policy allows proportionately more money for the appearance of their products.
— Japanese design policy allow for new ways to improve the appearance and visual quality (more progressive in design, more 'professional' look).
— Japanese products show a better and more expensive material choice and use, an all-over better technical-finish and production quality.'

The remainder of the document consisted of comparative photographs, with annotations which were not flattering to Philips. A typical comparison was between what were labelled a National Panasonic 3 Band portable radio and Philips top radio recorder. The comments on the Panasonic model were: 'Plastic cabinet with die-casted aluminium front panel rim. Aluminium deep drawn side panels. Aluminium trim glued on top and front panels, very refined production quality and sturdily mounted controls. Special triple indicator. Moving scale.' The comment on the Philips competitor stated: 'All plastic cabinet, partly silver sprayed and wood-printed (P. V. C. folie) inlays. Some knobs not in line with cabinet and not sturdily mounted. Sinkmarks in speaker boxes. Total cabinet gives a crackling noise when handled.' The message from all the examples was starkly clear: the Japanese were giving more detailed thought and attention to the visual appearance of their products, creating in comparison, through both visual and tactile means, a sense of substance and quality. The report was typical of several prepared within CIDC and presented to the Board of Management over several years in the 1970s, which emphasized the need for the company to compete on quality rather than cost.

Design Technique

Knut Yran placed great emphasis on drawing as a basic design skill and on rendering as a presentation technique. The latter could have a powerful visual impact and create a very attractive impression on clients and commissioners. The American designer and graphic artist Syd Mead, who could produce marvellous renderings, was a frequent visitor to CIDC to work on improving techniques and standards in this medium. Visuals, in this sense, played a key role in the concept of design techniques at CIDC under Yran (fig. 36).

Work was also progressing in Philips at this time, however, on the very different and radically new techniques of computer aided design (CAD). To explore its possibilities, in 1973, a working group including the industrial designer Fritz Zabransky, was established in the Centre for Technology, another of Philips Concern groups. Early work in CAD had been predominantly in the area of technical design, but the Philips group aimed to develop techniques applicable to the phase of product realization.

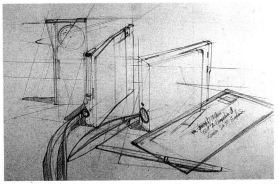

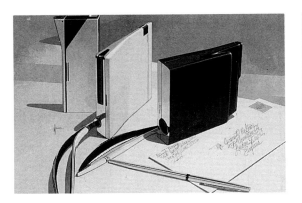

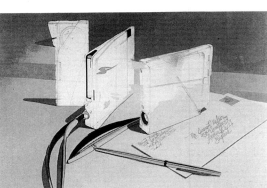

36. Presentation drawings showing the rendering effects developed by Syd Mead.

Management in CIDC

In any system of management the influence of personality is profound, particularly when the organization is focussed on a character as strong as Knut Yran. He was a man of powerful convictions, believing totally in the value of design and its potential contribution to both individual and social life. He was prepared to discuss problems, but he took all decisions. 'His word was law' was the comment of a designer who worked under him. He checked all designs before they were submitted to Product Divisions, insisting that they had to be worthy of carrying his signature since he bore the ultimate responsibility. Some designers who worked under him and reacted against his approach admit that it forced a high level of performance from them to justify their position.

Knut Yran introduced many initiatives which profoundly changed the role and nature of design at Philips. He was dynamic and enthusiastic, quick to defend his design staff, powerfully advocating the cause of design wherever possible. He particularly emphasized the need for presentation skills, especially drawing and rendering, to be raised to a higher levels of competence and provided the means to do it. He made considerable achievements within the vertical hierarchy, reporting directly to the Board of Management, leaving till later those developments in the area of lateral relationships on which the work of CIDC was to be increasingly dependent for its effectiveness. Due in considerable measure to his efforts, the range of work undertaken considerably expanded and the number of staff employed by CIDC grew between 1966-70 from 45 to 100 in The Netherlands centre alone, after which it stabilized. He wrote that it was necessary 'to invest in design like one invests in research and marketing, not only order it like the dessert with one or another special flavour.' Ultimately, the considerable growth of CIDC under his leadership, the extension of its role in Philips, the acceptance of it as a necessary element in overall strategic policy, must be seen as positive achievements which laid a foundation for the further developments of recent years.

PART 2

DESIGN FOR A GLOBAL MARKET

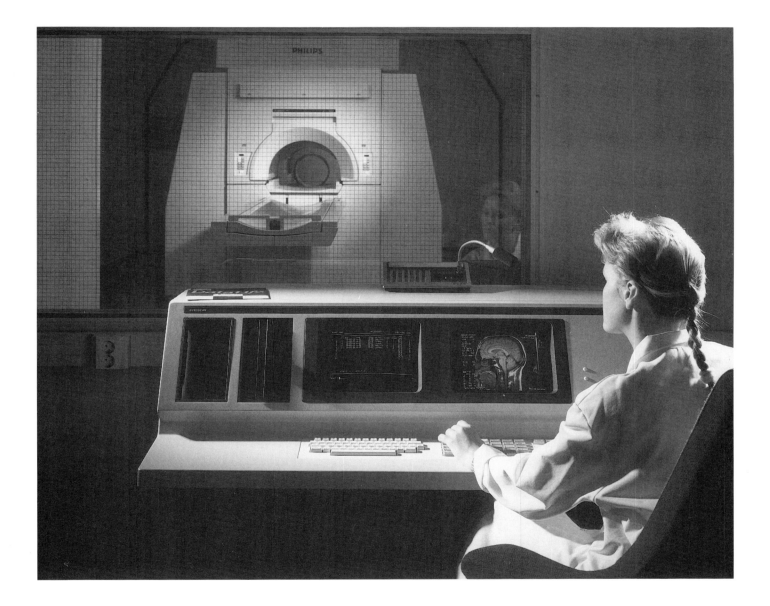

By the late 1970s, Philips Board of Management was concerned by the company's performance in key areas compared to many leading competitors, particularly from Japan and other Asian countries. The reasons were complex, but Dr. Wisse Dekker (fig. 37), then Vice-Chairman of the Board, believed there was a danger that Philips with its long traditions, could become institutionalized and inflexible in responding to changes in technology, production methods and markets. A process of re-structuring the company began which sought to shake-up the structure and free it from inhibiting rigidities. In particular, there was a need to shift the balance of power from the national organizations, which could operate almost as independent bodies, back to the product divisions with a new concept of global policy. In addition, emphasis was placed on devolving responsibility and accountability downwards, giving potential for and confidence in decision making to those best able to exercise it.

In 1980 Knut Yran reached retirement age and it became necessary to appoint a new Managing Director of CIDC. In considering the profile for the post, the Board of Management again decided the appointee should have a broad international orientation to match the range of Philips products and markets, with relevant experience in design and management. This could be in a totally different branch of industry, since design was regarded as a professional activity capable of flexible application. The net was cast world-wide for a suitable candidate.

In late 1980, Robert Blaich (fig. 38) was appointed to the post. Educated in his native

37. Dr. Wisse Dekker, President of Philips 1981 to 1986.

38. Robert Blaich.

39. Herman Miller designers, c. 1977: left to right, back row: Robert Propst, Robert Blaich, D.J. De Pree (founder), and Charles Eames, front row Alexander Girard, George Nelson, Ray Eames.

USA as an architect and industrial designer, he had worked for many years for Herman Miller Inc., a leading manufacturer of furnishing systems, which had employed some of the giants of modern design, such as Charles Eames and George Nelson (fig. 39). Blaich had risen to the post of Vice-President for Corporate Design and Communications, in charge of product development and all visual manifestations of the company. At one point he combined that post with Managing Director of Herman Miller/Europe for two years, based in Basle, Switzerland. He had thus gained considerable managerial experience before he left in 1979, to establish his own design/communications consulting company. This was beginning to be successful and when first approached about the possibility of working for Philips, Blaich was dubious. However, a conversation with Dr. Dekker in New York changed his mind, convincing him the post presented interesting possibilities. Subsequent visits to Eindhoven for in-depth discussions with a range of Philips top management confirmed his feeling that 'here was a company ready to make a move', which presented a challenge and the opportunity to respond to it. From the side of the company, it was felt he was capable of providing leadership in line with the new policy direction.

The company he entered in 1980 was a giant of the electrical industry, but in Blaich's opinion the focus on national organizations and local requirements had led to design resources being spread without real control, duplication of products and confusion in decision-making. 'Moreover', he later wrote in the STA Design Journal of 1986, 'the corporation's image in design and communications was very grey.'

Setting out the Stall

Soon after his arrival at Eindhoven, Blaich was invited to give a presentation to the Board of Management of his thoughts on how design at Philips should develop. He began by stating his belief that the design of any product or communication must above all satisfy the customer, citing criteria for evaluating user satisfaction. To make design a consistent factor in Philips future competitiveness, he proposed a strategy with four major elements, namely design policy, design management, improved professional standards, and an equal partnership for design.

These four points were the foundation stones of Blaich's approach to the re-organization of CIDC and were subsequently elaborated and detailed.

Design, Blaich has continually stated, is crucial to industrial and commercial competitiveness in any undertaking: 'The product', he emphasizes, 'is the most important statement a company can make about its image. It is the image.' However, if design was to play a significant role in Philips as a whole, a clear, coherent industrial design policy had to be established at corporate level, with the activities defined and consistently maintained throughout the company.

For design to be accepted as an effective competitive instrument it needed greater influence in management processes. To achieve this, however, the establishment and maintenance of industrial design itself had to be a managed process, with a coherent organizational structure and clearly defined responsibilities, relating to and compatible with the overall management structure of Philips.

Blaich also pointed out that demands on designers were rapidly changing. The design process could no longer be described simply in terms of a beginning and an end, it had become complex, evolutionary and on-going, no longer preoccupied with single objects and their aesthetics, but with an awareness that the environment must be designed holistically for it to be genuinely humane. If attitudes were to change and standards of design activity be improved and sustained at a high creative and professional level, a diverse and on-going programme of training and development was necessary.

Above all, for design to play a decisive role, it had to be integrated as an equal partner in the processes of development, production and marketing. To achieve this would not be easy, since in addition to designers taking new initiatives, it also required a similar response from other sectors of the company.

Blaich also stressed that to effectively assess designs and communicate ideas about them, an emphasis on individual, subjective values was insufficient. Instead there must exist a set of criteria against which design at Philips could be judged and he set out a check list of six, which were later incorporated into the formal design policy of CIDC. The checklist asked: is the product ergonomically designed to satisfy human factors, and is it intelligible; does the product not only meet minimum safety standards, but extend to anticipating potentially dangerous situations; does the product successfully solve a consumer need; is it compatible with its environment; is the product designed to utilize materials, production processes and energy in the most efficient way; and finally are aesthetic elements such as form, colours and textures as well as graphic information integrated in an appropriate manner.

These criteria signalled an important change of emphasis, from the inwardly-focussed professionalism of the Design Track to outwardly-focussed values stressing the constant testing of designs against the needs of commissioners and customers.

During the presentation, Blaich was asked by a Board member if the provision for design on the scale envisaged would not be expensive. 'What is the cost of no design?', he replied. In elaborating on that answer, he emphasized the product creation process as a strategic issue for the company. Although Philips cannot be characterized as design-led, design is a part of its strategic policy. As part of a team generating future products on which the company depends, design should not be considered a cost centre, Blaich argues, but rather as a profit centre. There is, in fact, a paradox in the nature of the factors constituting the 'added value' of a product, which make it attractive and competitive, for they are frequently non-price qualities stemming from the design function. Later in 1981, in a keynote speech to a symposium held at Philips domestic appliance headquarters at Groningen in the north of The Netherlands, Blaich summed up his beliefs: 'I believe that design is an integral part of the company's strategy and policy, that design decisions are as important as those of the commercial and production departments and that designers must be part of a team with commercial/technical and other relevant disciplines.'

Selling the potential of design at Board level to an audience convinced of its importance was relatively easy, however, compared to the problems of delivering on the promises. In retrospect Blaich recalls, 'My fear was that I might be over-selling. I was convincing top management we had all the marbles and then I looked here and saw we had some weaknesses.'

That was an understatement: the task facing him was huge. The scale of design activity at Philips was constantly increasing and design had become a truly multi-national activity. In early 1983, Philips had 194 designers and support staff of nineteen different nationalities, working in 30 locations in 20 countries. These broke down to 132 people in Europe, 36 in North and South America, and 26 in Asia. In 1982, a total of 632 projects of various scale and complexity were completed, increasing to 750 in 1983, 1,150 in 1984, and 1,360 in 1985. By 1987, the figure was over 2000. In addition, in an average year the CIDC Graphics and Packaging service completes over 200 jobs in packaging, advertising and point-of-sale design, direct mail and promotional literature. All these commissions originated from product divisions' requests for design work on new and existing products, and requests from National Organizations for assistance on locally developed products. Designers from CIDC were sometimes seconded to satellite centres for special projects. In one year, for example, personnel from CIDC worked on designs for refrigerators and domestic appliances in Mexico, radio recorders, HiFi and portables in India, and shavers and small domestic appliances in Japan.

Organization and Delegation

Robert Blaich is emphatic that the design function in a company such as Philips must have a structure and policy objectives consonant with the structure and policy of the company as whole. The latter were undergoing substantial change, however, in the period of Blaich's appointment. Under the direction of Dr. Wisse Dekker, Chairman of the Board of Management from 1982 to 1986, and his successor Cor van der Klugt (fig. 40), the structure of the company has shifted away from the matrix system established in 1946 and the dual leadership of technical and commercial management derived from the founding brothers. Dr. Dekker changed the emphasis from technology and national organizations to a market driven, user-oriented policy of globalization. This opened possibilities for considerable change in the organization and role of designers. Cor van der Klugt, whilst continuing the process of change, has also been highly supportive of the role of design in the company. When he was Vice-Chairman of the Board of Management CID had reported to him, and he often visited the Design Center for personal reviews during which he made a strong impression with his detailed comments and many suggestions for improvements. 'Van der Klugt is a real product man', says Robert Blaich. This level of understanding and support from the highest levels of Philips has undoubtedly been a very significant factor in establishing an appropriate climate in which design policy could develop.

There were some fundamental problems to be addressed. 'One of the myths,' says Blaich, 'was that the company had to design products for every different country. We attacked it here internally, it was a design initiative and we were able to point out that this was a lot of nonsense. First of all if that was true, how were the Japanese getting such a stranglehold on Europe? Secondly, as a result, designers were sitting in factories and taking orders from the technology or commercial people. The product divisions did not control their destiny because of the national organizations' power.'

40. Cor van der Klugt, President of Philips since 1986.

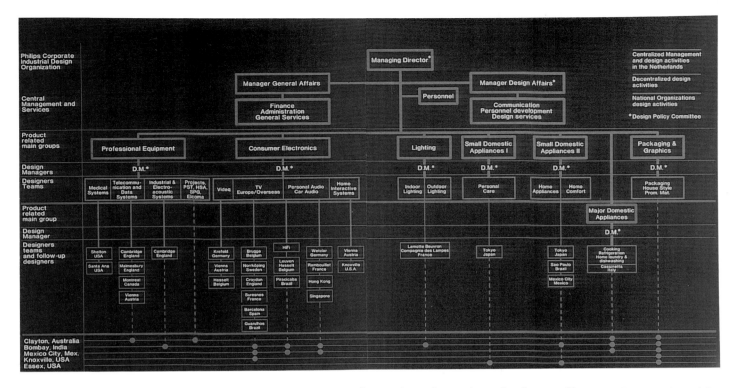

A further problem was the lack of adequate communication and interaction between product divisions. This resulted in considerable opportunities being missed. For example, a division developing the video recorder kept it as a technical product, so it was never fully developed for the consumer area. Even within product divisions, vertical separation resulted in product areas becoming virtually autonomous, each with its own design ideas.

To solve such problems, however, a clear priority on appointment for Robert Blaich was to establish a managerial structure for the design function, enabling decisions to be effectively made and executed. On arrival at Philips, Blaich found some twenty-five people reported directly to him, a situation emphasizing control rather than implementation. The scale of change required could not be devised overnight, however, it needed careful planning and consultation. His first step was to talk to people, evaluate the organization and establish the balance of strengths and weaknesses. His experience convinced him that a company with Philips scale of operations required both effective organization and delegation.

Immediately after taking up his post, Blaich organized a series of meetings for key staff, focussing on the role of design within the total Philips structure and then turning to the internal organization of the design function itself. The emphasis was on opportunities for clarifying this function both in its vertical relationships with top management and its lateral relationships with those in other sectors of the company who commissioned work. As a result, by the end of 1981, the first outlines began to emerge for a new organizational structure (fig. 41). At the same time Philips commissioned an Overhead Value Analysis, in the central corporation, to analyze the role, cost-effectiveness and aims of each area and the work of each member of staff, which was then checked against overall needs. The results of this independent survey, for CIDC, confirmed the in-house analysis. Discussions with commissioning agencies in the company provided a clearer view of their requirements.

The publication of the new structure in March, 1982, emphasized the need for 'change to more effectively deal with change' (fig. 42). The declared goals of the reorganization were to create clearer lines of responsibility and authority, to increase involvement in decision mak-

41. Diagram of new CID organizational structure, since slightly extended.

ing by line and staff personnel and to improve and focus project management. The plan also allowed for clearer career planning and personal growth for employees, for managing design research, and within that reducing indirect costs.

The operational scheme of 1969, which the new organization replaced, had three levels: at the top was the director, with his personal assistants and secretaries; the second was a substantial staff level including such functions as finance, administration and information; the final level consisted of a series of design groups with group leaders in charge. The new organizational concept grouped and simplified the staff functions of support services and administration, placing them under the control of a Manager for Design Affairs who also acted as deputy to the Director. Frans van der Put was appointed to this post and his long experience of Philips has been invaluable in implementing new policies. Blaich is warm in his tributes to the contribution made by van der Put: 'I couldn't have succeeded without him', he says, 'Frans is the glue around here, he makes things stick.' The two men come from different backgrounds, with very different

personalities, but in a real sense they complement each other and form a highly effective partnership.

The most radical organizational innovation was the creation of new posts of Design Manager for each major product sector: professional equipment, consumer electronics, major domestic appliances, small domestic appliances, personal care, light, with in addition, packaging and graphics, which crossed all product sectors (fig. 43). Each Design Manager had a brief to achieve the closest possible co-operation with their Product Division and had direct line responsibility to the Managing Director, Design. 'I want to manage the design process,' says Blaich, 'not manage the designers. Each one of them has to run their own area, and I will direct and support them, but I'm not going to be involved in every day to day activity.' The Design Managers were therefore given full responsibility for their own area. The introduction of the title 'Design Manager' was a deliberate choice, a key criterion being that each holder of the position should be selected for their capacity to assume managerial responsibility, in addition to other factors such as creativity, tech-

42. Diagram of organizational structure based on geographical locations.

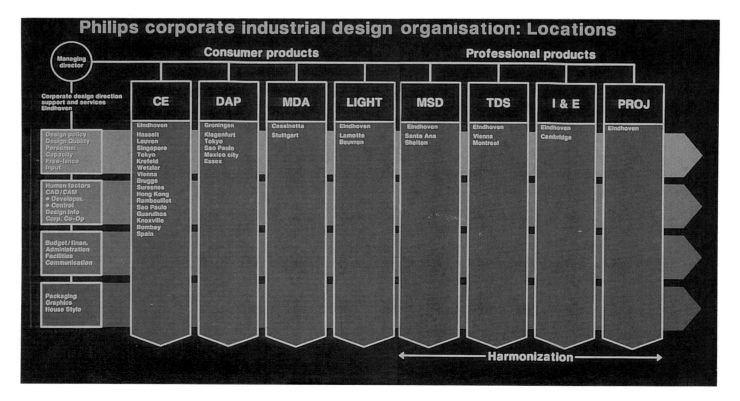

43. Philips Design Managers from left to right: (standing) Frans van der Put, Andre Rotte, Huug Sterkenburg, Henk Schellens, Johnny Lippinkhof; (seated) Peter Nagelkerke, Robert Blaich, Lou Beeren, Jo Rosenbaum. Stefano Marzano is not included.

nical expertise and experience. Whilst in retrospect that might seem obvious, it had not previously been the case. It therefore became necessary to identify people with the requisite managerial ability or potential. 'So throughout the organization I looked for the people who I felt were the most qualitative and could grow', says Blaich. A major criterion was that design managers should be capable of bridging gulfs between product groups by using design as a link. In some cases the search for the right person meant giving accelerated promotion to young people who then had authority over those to whom they had previously been assistant. It was the start of a campaign to involve the Design Managers fully in creating a new consciousness of design — top down, bottom up, and sideways.

The devolution of control downwards was also important in allowing design managers to adapt to the varying and changing circumstances of their area of responsibility. Hugo Sterkenberg, in charge of Medical Systems I and E (fig. 44), and of special projects, comments: 'It's a continuous process of learning from decisions taken in the past, adjusting the rules, and meeting new market requirements.' His work varies from

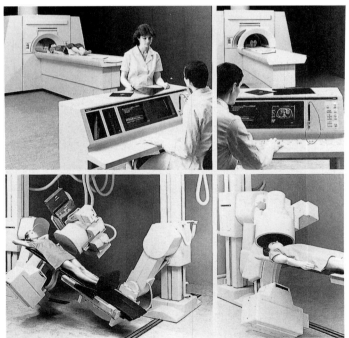

the emphasis on commonality in the Harmonisation Programme to highly specific projects such as a Motorway Traffic Control and Signalling System for the Dutch Government. In Consumer Products, Peter Nagelkerke had to deal with highly personalized articles, such as

44. The results of the harmonization programme in medical products.

45. Product range of shavers over the years.

46. A microwave oven one of Philips major domestic appliances.

47. The CID logo introduced in 1985.

at Cassinetta in Italy, similarly believes design must be put on a more professional level: 'at the beginning of every PROCO [Product Committee] meeting, I always start the presentation with background information about the trends that influenced the product design. Along with these ideas I present the methodology involved in the design process' (fig. 46). Not only the range of ideas but the quality of initiatives originating from the design managers has immeasurably strengthened the lateral links with other disciplines in the product divisions.

The shake-up, and shake-out, resulting from the reorganization was absolutely necessary, Blaich believes, not only from the point of view of organizational efficiency, but to revive morale amongst the designers. 'Many designers here,' he observes, 'accepted their secondary role but in reality deeply resented it, and as a result we had lost many good people in the past.'

As a co-ordinating and policy-making body, the Design Policy Committee was established under the chairmanship of the Managing Director, CIDC, on which the Manager for Design Affairs and all Design Managers sat. This body was established to deal with on-going matters of design policy and to provide a review function for the work of the design teams. Rather than the weekly review of all projects previously used by DESTA, however, each major product area has a major review of its total performance every six months, with the form of the review left to Design Managers to determine.

As a further measure to ensure closer contact with the product divisions, fifteen contact designers, with line responsibility to the Design Managers, were appointed for specific product areas, such as video display systems, home en-

shavers (fig. 45) and now products for more general use such as television, each having their own emphasis. He sees his role as establishing a smooth running organization so he has time for 'inspiring people and supporting them in their work'. This extends to some highly structured and thought provoking theoretical work with which to back up design arguments. Stefano Marzano, of Major Domestic Appliances, based

tertainment systems, home information systems, or personal and car audio. They have charge of the day-to-day activities of a team including product designers, product graphic designers and support assistants.

In 1985, the title of CIDC, which referred specifically to the design centre located in Eindhoven, was altered to Corporate Industrial Design (CID), a change encompassing all Philips design activities and intended to reflect the globality of the industrial design function worldwide (fig. 47).

Design Policy

By 1984 the Design Policy Committee had prepared a definitive statement of design policy for publication. It began with a statement on CID's 'responsibility for the industrial design function and quality for Philips worldwide, from a corporate as well as a line function point of view.' This was to be achieved in four ways. Firstly, CID was to develop the corporate visual image, functioning as a 'connector' between the products, product systems and packaging of the Product Divisions, to create a strong visual image for all Philips products. A second responsibility was meeting users' expectations, as CID had specific skills in giving visual expression to products, which should 'satisfy the expectations and sensibilities of the ultimate users of Philips products.' Thirdly there was meeting production and marketing requirements, by which designers were responsible for integrating these requirements into design work. Finally, CID was to be continually defining product design quality, emphasizing qualitative factors in design, as well as developing criteria and a continuing dialogue to increase understanding of these factors throughout the organization.

Another feature of the designers' remit is the need for 'continuous, optimal communication with all Product Divisions on product planning, policy, development and marketing'. However, if CID has responsibilities, the policy statement also proposes a formal status for design in the process of product development which broke new ground in the company. Whilst industrial design functioned as part of an interdisciplinary team, it is emphasized that its expertise was contributed on a basis of equality with other participating disciplines. This was summarized in a diagram devised by Frans van der Put, in which successful product development was depicted as a three-way relationship of equality between design, development production and marketing, each capable of its unique contribution (fig. 48). To ensure industrial design quality is maintained 'as an integral part of the total quality of a product, product system, or packaging', evaluation has to be included in the development process. The statement is a clear indication that in terms of policy, the days when design could be regarded as a last resort for styling exercises are over.

The policy document was deliberately concise, for elaborate statements can lead to confusion, and in any case are no substitute for action. Nevertheless, it gave clear commitment to a series of changes, some already achieved,

48. The model of the design function devised by Frans van der Put.

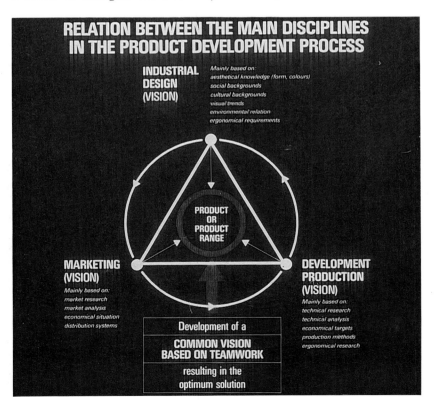

43

others underway, which represented a wholly new function and image for design within the Philips organization.

The responsibility of the Design Policy Committee did not, of course, end with the publication of the policy document, since it has an ongoing strategic responsibility for design. Its activities are intended to provide professional guidance for design quality, which it does by means of design reviews, and to interpret long term corporate requirements for product design quality and planning in terms of specific policy and its implementation.

The DPC thus has to be flexible in its response to development both within the company and outside. In 1984 it published a revision of the organizational structure which reflected the mounting pace of change both in CID and the company as a whole. Change in the organization of product divisions was an important factor, resulting from the awareness of technical and functional overlap in many areas, with the need to integrate new concepts of design, development and marketing also playing a part. An obvious corollary was to realign the organization of CID design groups to match those developments.

The problems of decentralized design groups over which there was little control has been referred to earlier and a remedy was obviously necessary if control and coordination over all Philips design activities was to be effective. Therefore in a second major change of policy decentralized design groups within the company were brought into closer relationships with CID and the national organization design groups were linked in closer consultation. This was yet another step in establishing a unified approach across the whole Philips organization.

Design and Engineering

Efforts to promote the role and achievement of designers in Philips, however, demanded that the vexed question of the boundaries between the roles of engineering and industrial design be addressed. Any jealous feeling that a professional preserve was being encroached on could result in unnecessary obstacles to the product development process and hamper the possibility of fruitful co-operation with product divisions. Recognizing this, Robert Blaich tackled the problem head-on at the highest level. In 1983 he addressed the annual joint meeting of the Board of Management and the heads of the National Organizations, the annual Philips managerial 'summit', at Ouchy, Switzerland; this was the first time a head of design had been invited to make a presentation. He gave a comparison of their respective methodologies. Engineers, he argued, are trained to solve problems by thinking in terms of technical details and work from those details, from the inside of a product outward. In comparison, industrial designers normally work from the outside in. Their thinking starts with the complete product as it would be used by someone, working back into the details of how to make the concept work. Engineers are concerned with the interaction of components and materials and are responsible for ensuring a product will work. They should develop the best product consistent with the state of technology and anticipated market price. Industrial designers, on the other hand, must ensure a product will by bought by making its use-value perceivable and sustaining that image by convenience of use in practice.

Both disciplines, argued Blaich, are now less interested in individual products and more in systems. There too, however, differences of approach need to be acknowledged. Engineers must view a system as a series of products and components capable of being related in various configurations through technical compatibility. Whilst these configurations are also of interest to designers, they must also be concerned with related systems of graphics, packaging, marketing and above all, the mechanics of operations by users and groups of users. The work of engineer and industrial designer was therefore described in terms of complementarity and should, he concluded, be regarded collaboratively.

Globalization

The concept of systems was of fundamental importance in defining the new policies of CID. Robert Blaich frequently pointed to the growth in importance of 'universal' products and systems and stressed the need for Philips industrial design policies to be re-oriented from individual products to systems and co-ordinated programmes, shifting from locally designed products for local markets in national organizations to world market concepts. In reviewing progress in the year 1984 in the CID house-journal, he wrote: 'For global design management, the most important tools are a clear design policy and program for quality control.'

In taking up the theme of globality, Blaich emphasizes both centralization and decentralization as necessary and compatible, acknowledging in this the ideas of Thomas Watson of IBM. In 1980 CID was decentralized but not controlled. Blaich argues that products for specific markets and cultural needs can be directed from a central point of view, and conversely, to emphasize local needs too much can restrict the potential market and application of a product. He cites the Tracer electric razor as an example of the latter (fig. 49). On his arrival at CID the design group in Japan was designing a shaver for Japanese people. The criteria were: it should be small because their hands were small, it should be portable since the Japanese have a great enthusiasm for portable goods, for example with Walkman type products; and, it was argued, the shaving head did not have to be so strong because Japanese do not have heavy beards. A small two-headed shaver for the Japanese market, answering these criteria, emerged. The Commercial Department, however, questioned whether it was solely a 'Japanese' product. 'They thought it might be suitable for young people everywhere, says Blaich, 'they too have light beards and are on the move with their Walkman on their hip.' It was test marketed in Australia and the Tracer emerged. There was some fear it might steal market share from the **three-headed Philishave, but instead it has been a huge success in opening up new markets amongst young people.**

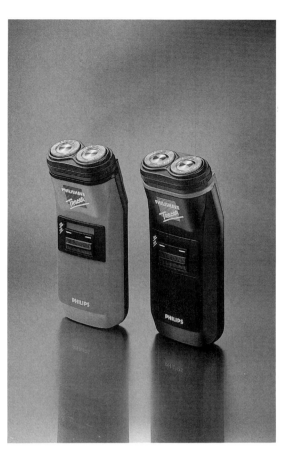

49. The Tracer electric shaver (see also product study, page 79).

The case of the Tracer is highly illustrative of the possibility of globalizing in terms of segmenting the horizontal bands of user categories, such as age, or life-style, which exist across the world. It promoted the development of the Roller Radio and Moving Sound range of audio equipment for young people (fig. 50). Segmenting can, however, also be in terms of vertical divisions of nationality or culture, for example, with equipment such as rice cookers and coffee machines, where differences in taste and the way items are prepared require a totally different product. The concept of targeting specific markets on the basis of standard elements has led to many initiatives which have been design led, such as the GR1 television (fig. 51). This is a product which anticipates globality in appearance, but which has to be adaptable to the differing TV systems across the world. 'We have to play both ends of this thing and be flexible,'

50. the Moving Sound
product range (see also
product study, page 135)

51. The GRI television
set.

says Blaich, 'within standardization there is the possibility of infinite diversity.'

Globalism is now a key element in Philips response to the challenges of a demanding and competitive world. In a definition of global strategy in a speech given at Harvard University, the Chairman of the Board of Management, Cor van der Klugt, stated: 'A global strategy will be directed by a centralized policy and planning process. Product planning, design, development and global marketing strategy will be integrated into a coherent centralized process.' He went on to identify three key markets in which the company will concentrate its efforts, Europe, the USA and the Pacific Basin/China. The centralization of design resources was a necessary response to this policy in terms of making specialist competences available throughout the company. More recently, the various design units throughout the world have been gradually concentrated into three 'Centres of Competence' corresponding to the three zone concept outlined by Cor van der Klugt. The changes involved in adapting to the new structure and concepts again requires adaptability and creative response from CID. Its recent history, however, can perhaps be summarised in terms of the management of and response to change.

House Style

Further problems arising from the scale of organization in the company were also an important consideration in the renewed attention given to the application of the Philips House style in 1984. The House Style Manual had first been introduced in 1973, but the complex international structure of Philips and widespread autonomous practice created problems in sus-

taining a recognizable identity (fig. 52). 'There were very tight rules about house style but in fact most people ignored them', says Robert Blaich. 'Essentially the House Style Council was a policing activity. We were always writing letters to people telling them they had done it wrong instead of telling them how to do it right. When we went back and studied the rules we found a lot of them too complicated and duplicating themselves, so we simplified it'.

The company's House Style council, chaired by Robert Blaich, on which CID is represented together with the departments of Standardization, Patents & Trademarks, and Corporate Advertising, held a series of workshops and issued publications to remedy the situation. To help increase consciousness of essential points, the emphasis was on a simple check-list of basic points: six rules and three elements. The six rules established guidelines for use of housemarks, the Philips name and the stars and waves trademark, relating to prominence, clear

zones, proportion, alignment, similarity and legibility. The three house style elements set standard specifications for colour, typeface and basic layout or grids.

The rules and elements have been published in a folder which has been disseminated throughout the organization and gives a simple outline of these essential features (fig. 53). A full manual is also available for the purposes of detailed execution, giving specifications for such applications as transport, directional and information signs and wall plates, printed matter and exhibitions.

Without control and common practice, there is no possibility of establishing the house style as a marketing device, to sell the company and create an image. The problems of creating such conditions are rendered more difficult, however, by the use of a range of brand names under which similar Philips products are marketed in various parts of the world. These include Marantz in Japan, Radiola in France and Bauknecht in Germany. The situation is particularly complicated in the USA, where Magnavox, Syl-

52. An example of how not to present the Philips name.

53. The new, simplified house style manual.

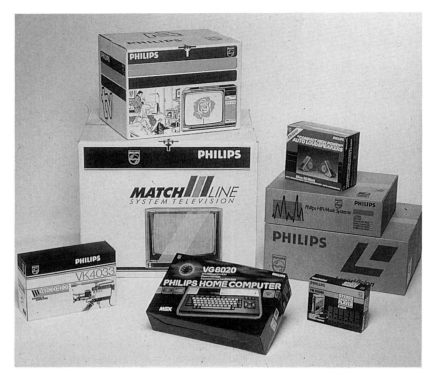

vania, Norelco and Philco are also used. Blaich had predicted that brand names will become more specific to market groups rather than countries, but he accepts that it is a complex problem to which there is no quick or easy solution.

There has been considerable change, however. 'We have moved the house style to be much more market oriented,' says Blaich. As a result, the complete Philips packaging programme in consumer products areas and professional product areas has been harmonized, in the belief that packaging is an extension of the product, and should therefore be integral to the product concept (fig. 54). A further step is to consider products at point of sale. This has frequently been a point of breakdown in image creation, since national organizations with their own advertising staff could go in their own direction. Recent initiatives have addressed the problem and there are now coordinated pro-

54. Packaging for consumer electronic products before and after redesign.

grammes into the point of sale, which are beginning to have an effect. Another area for consideration was advertising, where similar problems existed, with a plethora of advertising agencies across the world doing work for Philips. The problems there are not easily solved but a breakthrough came when the Consumer Electronics Division decided to develop a coherent programme, resulting in a highly successful series of advertisements adapted for use in many countries and languages. Blaich is a member of the Advertising Policy Board, the only non-divisional member, and finds it helps CID to contribute to major programmes of universal packaging and advertising.

The cumulative effect of all these endeavours is to move the concept of house style from a limited concept of marks that have patent value, to a totally integrated image for Philips in which product, packaging, point-of-sale display and advertising all complement each other and work to the same end, giving a coherent impression of quality in every aspect. Blaich wants to change

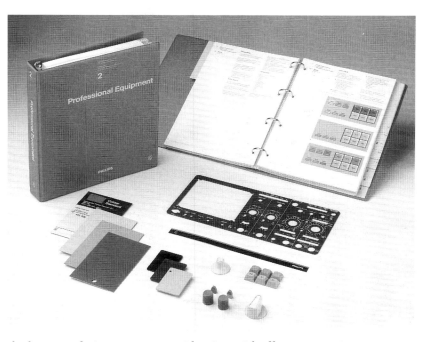

the house style into a corporate identity, with all disciplines contributing (fig. 55). There is some way to go before that ideal is reached, but important steps have been taken along the road.

55. The harmonization manual for Professional Equipment.

Improving Standards – Press for the Best

If design is to be accepted on an equal footing with other disciplines, the skills designers can bring to the processes of product development and marketing have to be clarified. Modern practitioners, Robert Blaich argues, require knowledge and capability in a wide spectrum of fields: engineering, aesthetics, graphic design, computer science, market research and ergonomics, both physical and psychological, in order to practice their own professional skills and also in order to have an effective dialogue with colleagues in other disciplines. Above all, since product intelligibility is of critical importance in market success, industrial designers have to know how to communicate clearly, so that users find products comprehensible, accessible and pleasurable.

On all these levels an on-going programme of professional development embracing all staff and activities within CID has been a constant concern for Robert Blaich and the Design Managers. It takes many forms, indeed variety is

necessary to meet diverse needs effectively and maintain the possibility of genuine stimulus. Some elements of the programme have a very specific professional application, but others can be highly speculative. Their common intent is to stimulate fresh thinking.

Inviting visitors to inject new ideas from outside the company is perhaps one of the most obvious means. They were used in the early days of Blaich's directorship to stimulate the review of operational procedures within CID, and have since been a constant feature. Leading figures are invited to present papers on their work and ideas, and to emphasize that stimulus can equally well come from inside the company, members of CID and other Philips divisions also give presentations on new ideas.

Amongst early visitors was Niels Diffrient from the USA, who stressed two themes. One was the shift from 'styling only design' to 'total concept design', from design as an afterthought in the product development process, to design-

56. The participants at a recent lighting workshop, from CID as well as from outside consultancies. (Left to right, back row: David Gresham (Design Logic, Chicago), Gus Rodriguez (CID), Mark Armstrong (Blue Sky Design, Sydney), Jean-Francois Arnaud (SAMI, Annecy), Robert Kohler (Kohler Rekow, Paris), Tom Newhouse (Thomas J. Newhouse Design, Grand Rapids), Oscar Pena (CID), Steef Joosten (CID), Don Waslander (CID), Bill Moggridge (ID Two, San Francisco) and front row Menno Dieperink (CID) and **Henk Schellens (CID).**

ing integrated with management, engineering, manufacturing and marketing. This clearly paralleled current CID thinking. Diffrient's second theme was the development of systematic ergonomic data as a design tool during the time he worked for Henry Dreyfuss Associates in New York. The value of such presentations in raising consciousness of the need for change was reflected in discussion, when staff felt that more data had to be gathered and applied to improve the ergonomic performance of Philips products. The realization that a problem existed, however, was not enough for Blaich. An important factor in invitations to outside visitors was his belief that formal presentations also needed a

follow-up, wherever possible, to explore the implications of valuable ideas and possibilities of implementing them. Accordingly, later in the same year, Diffrient returned for a week's consultancy, exploring the application of both themes in his original presentation to practical problems.

The list of workshops which have now taken place at CID is becoming lengthy and outside consultants are still used as concept generators. Another aspect of consultancy, however, is where outside expertise not readily available at CID is brought in for work on a specific project, for example, the Philips Electronic Office System. They usually work with staff from CID,

whose designers thereby have an opportunity to absorb new ideas and methods. There is a limit, however, to the range of work on which outside consultants can be used. Some product concepts are so sensitive and the need for secrecy so great that access is highly restricted. Nevertheless, a considerable range of people have visited CID in the role of teachers and educators in a broad sense. In some cases it is possible to show products that have resulted from the contact, but more important, Blaich believes, is the resulting change in attitudes (fig. 56)

In a report to CID staff in early 1983, Robert Blaich wrote: 'We know that the market realities dictated by the most difficult economic climate in the postwar period will require us to be the best that we can be. This means that each of us individually must convert problems into opportunities, frustrations into positive action, ideas into products. We must constantly test ourselves and our abilities against these challenges. If we can develop these positive attitudes we can together contribute an important and critically necessary service to Philips.' Behind the exhortatory tone lay a clear recognition that structures and programmes for information and training alone were not enough. If the critical levels of quality needed to sustain Philips competitiveness were to be achieved and maintained, attitudes had to change.

A key element in nurturing talent is by challenging orthodoxies, opening up discussion and constantly encouraging alternative views, and in this respect Robert Blaich leads from the front. In his first column in the CID house-journal, *inForm* of June, 1981, he reviewed the catalogue of an exhibition 'Bakelite' at the Boymans-van Beunigen Museum in Rotterdam, containing many early Philips products, and also an article in the Italian design journal *Domus*, featuring drawings of the technological fantasies of Michele de Lucchi, a founder of Memphis, the avant-garde design group based in Milan. De Lucchi argued that technological development now allowed an almost total concealment of mechanical function. This challenged the doctrine associated with the Modern Movement of the 1920s, and in particular with the German design school, the Bauhaus, that

mechanical function should be the determinant of form in design. Known as the 'Functionalist' approach, this became the dominant ideology in European design education and practice in the post-war years and also made deep inroads in the USA and other parts of the world. In contrast, wrote Blaich, 'Michele de Lucchi proposes that the form no longer be the servant of the mechanisms, but an active stimulus of perceptive imagination, so that (quoting de Lucchi) 'the machine loses its metallic appearance of hostile animosity and becomes the tactful and trusting friend of man.'

'Outrageous thinking?', queried Blaich. 'Yes, possibly, but look beyond the drawings. What did I see in common in the products in the Bakelite exhibit and the concept of de Lucchi? 1. Both were ahead of their time. 2. Both involve use of materials in a new and unexpected way. 3. Both propose to deliver joy, not only in the product, but in the form.' He invited staff to review both articles, suggesting 'Perhaps one man's fantasy is another's reality.' By challenging the tenets of Functionalism and suggesting that emotional response had a part to play, he encouraged a more flexible concept of what could be appropriate in Philips design. He rejects the concept of a Philips 'style' in formal terms, believing that with such a large and diverse range of products and markets a spectrum of approaches are desirable and necessary.

The example of the de Lucchi article led in fact to another workshop in 1985 on the subject of product semantics, a theory adapted from linguistics, which is concerned with how form and shape communicates. Klaus Krippendorff of the University of Pennsylvania, Reinhard Butter from Ohio State University, Michael and Katherine McCoy from Cranbrook Academy of Art and Uri Friedlaender, a product designer based in London presented papers on the subject and worked with CID participants, developing models exploring practical implications of the theories (fig. 57). As a stimulus it was highly successful, with an opportunity to let imagination play in manner rarely possible on commissions. More importantly it raised fundamental questions about possible ways in which the nature of products can be identified and

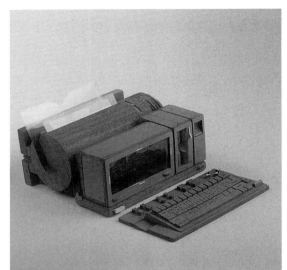

57. A 'Beethoven Radio' developed at a Product Semantics workshop, and semantics development work on the Video-Writer and on a video camera.

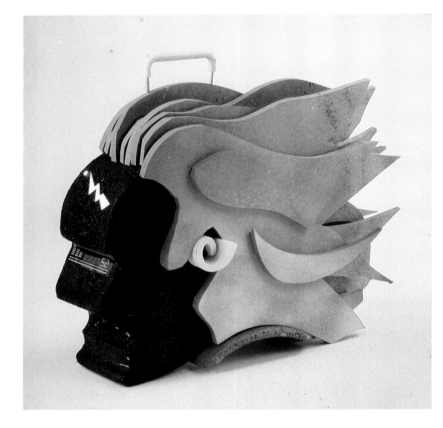

their function and purpose made self-evident to a user.

Blaich's challenge to conventional attitudes was not restricted to problems of form, but to a still prevalent image of designers as gifted, willful individuals – artists manque – whose talents could only be realized in conditions of freedom, of romantic isolation. In contrast, in a speech at the London Business School in January 1984, Blaich stressed his belief that 'innovation typically occurs in the interface of multiple disciplines . . . '. If the attitudes associated with 'styling' and of designers as somewhat raffish arbiters of 'taste' were to be altered, then designers' role as practitioners in a multidisciplinary context had to carry conviction with colleagues in other disciplines.

The achievement of such changes within CID, however, had to be within existing staffing provision and turnover rate, since budgetary policy did not allow for expansion. Therefore, in November, 1982, a small committee of three senior members of CID was set up to consider the question of renewal for all staff. A report with a policy statement on a comprehensive programme for 'professional renewal' was published the following year. It began with a detailed survey of the pattern of employment within CID, including an analysis of growth and age patterns, a survey of reasons why recently departed staff had resigned, and the expected retirement pattern across the next decade. Anticipated and potential changes in the factors affecting design, in disciplines such as Human Factors and CAD/CAM, were surveyed to provide a profile of what competences would be required. There followed a review of recruitment and renewal policies, to ensure a flow of new talent and provide existing staff with adequate opportunities for development and full career opportunities. In this respect an important section of the document specified the functions of designers at different levels, with criteria for evaluation so everyone knew what was required of them, as part of a strengthened procedure for selection, appointment and career planning. The conclusions emphasized the need for new, stimulating experiences, with workshops and special projects to introduce and up-date ideas and techniques. Rotation within the design organization was cited as a means of providing fresh perspectives and continually re-invigorating the organization.

The report was a model of its kind and typifies the management of CID, in thoroughly discussing relevant considerations supported by substantial evidence, and establishing a defined policy framework as a guide to action. The evaluation system provides a means of identifying performance and growth potential amongst staff; the establishment of training programmes and supervision of staff is clearly identified as a responsibility of Design Managers. An in-house programme of development through workshops and seminars has opened new perspectives and generated numerous practical ideas. In addition, personnel have participated in a wide range of relevant educational activities paid for by CID, ranging from international management to language and special skill courses. Robert Blaich estimates that 95% of the proposals in the report have been fully implemented. 'We had to show the staff that renewal didn't mean everybody was going to get their head lopped off', he commented, 'Now they believe in it.'

The ever-increasing scale of design activity presents difficulties for such a programme, yet at the same time constant renewal is imperative if standards of quality are to be maintained, let alone raised. A continuing problem has been products emanating from 'satellite' designers. Robert Blaich believes everyone involved in creative processes needs to draw continually on a range of resources to stimulate ideas, indeed, to even know what questions to ask. This, however, is difficult to sustain in isolation. 'All my experience tells me' he wrote, 'that creative designers are strengthened by their association

with other designers; they react to the creativity going on around them.' Therefore, he concluded, the isolation and independent management of 'satellite' designers must reflect on the quality of their work. The problem is how to maintain CID standards, whilst respecting the integrity of genuine local differences and needs.

Considerable efforts are made to link decentralized design groups to the central management of CID. The few remaining national organization design groups (still necessary because of closed market conditions), whilst focussing on the particular product ranges of their countries, are increasingly involved in consultation and co-ordination with CID. In practical terms, this means initiatives such as the 'guest designer' programme, with members of Philips design groups around the world brought to Eindhoven to work for varying periods, in order to intensify contact and communications and share information about concepts being explored at CID. In addition, a considerable portion of Robert Blaich's time each year is spent travelling to Philips design offices and production centres across the world, to maintain close, personal contact and coordinate developments.

An idea intended to address the problems of Philips designers being so widely distributed, and working on such a broad spectrum of product types, was a two-day meeting of what was titled the design Audio Research Team (DART), held in conjunction with the Japanese Audio Fair in 1983 at the factory for Philips audio in Japan, Marantz. In introducing it, Robert Blaich explained that alternative methods were needed to overcome the problems of a dispersed organization. The fourteen participants, drawn from across the organization, included not only designers but also staff from technical and commercial disciplines, yet again underlining the need for colleagues from different disciplines to focus on common problems and potential. The opening sessions introduced themes and trends, feeding in information, data, market perceptions and emerging technologies relevant to the field of HiFi and audio, followed by creative working sessions to produce specific design concepts. These were dis-

58. The Concept Car presented at the Turin Motor Show developed with IAD.

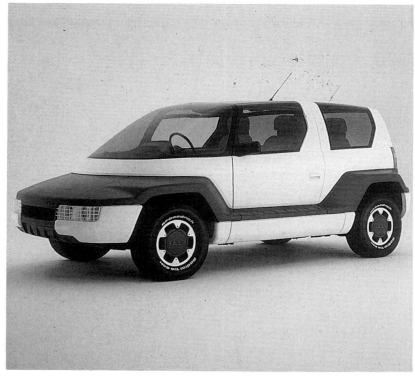

cussed and assessed and the most promising developed in more detail on the second day and presented to management of HiFi. Subsequent DART workshops were held in Knoxville in 1984 and Las Vegas in 1985. The idea of focussing the talents of staff from many countries on specific projects, in the context of major trade fairs whilst the stimulus of new developments was still fresh in the mind, led to valuable exchanges and the generation of numerous ideas subsequently introduced into production. DART reports have also proved useful when given to staff in other divisions as a tool to stimulate thinking amongst colleagues from other disciplines. The DART concept aroused so much interest that the format has been taken up in some product divisions.

In addition to such schemes, design research is being supported, with a portion of CID's budget committed to experimental projects. An example is a modular radio and in-car entertainment system for a British concept car, which aroused considerable interest when introduced at the Turin motor show in 1988 (fig. 58). Pre-development work on projects in order to accurately establish a body of relevant information and procedures is also being actively encouraged. This can be particularly important, for with ground work already completed, work on projects can be more accurately targeted whilst at the same time being considerably speeded up. Workshops held with professional cameramen in the pre-development stage of a new video camera design, resulted in a radically altered design concept (fig. 59).

The problem of how to keep a staff of some 240 people vital, involved and performing at a high level is, of course, a constant and on-going challenge. The recognition, however, that the collective creative talent of designers is a vitally important resource that needs nurturing, motivating and successfully harnessing if its potential is to be realized, is crucial to design management policy and practice. The process of raising standards directly contributes to the effectiveness of the design function in the company as a whole, in terms that can be tangible and even quantifiable. But there are also wider, long-term benefits in laying firm foundations for the future.

Within CID the processes of evaluation and renewal are already resulting in new design management talent emerging from the ranks of staff recruited as designers. In addition, a major push has been to recruit the best talent graduating from design schools across the world, and to train and develop their abilities. The recognition of designer Graham Hinde's concept of the Roller Radio and its evolution into one of Philips best-selling products is the most spectacular fruit of this approach (fig. 60), but there are other, on-going benefits which will ensure a flow of the best young designers to CID. Frans van der Put recalls his teachers telling him in the mid-1950s that he was too good for Philips. CID now has schools coming to it that previously were ignorant or antipathetic, wanting to know about it, to cooperate with it and encouraging their students to join it. It is difficult to imagine a more appropriate compliment to the success of CID's policies for raising standards.

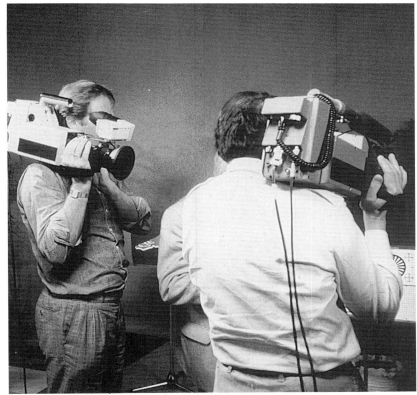

59. Development work on a professional video camera (see also product study page 130)

60. The Roller Radio (see also product study page 135)

Developing New Techniques

Another aspect of maintaining levels of quality and innovation is developing and adapting new techniques and concepts to aid designers in their work. Two areas of current significance in modern design are Computer Aided Design (CAD) and Applied Ergonomics, sometimes termed Human Factors.

CID'S involvement in Computer Aided Design (CAD) dates back to 1973 and has involved several departments and specialisms. Although considerable progress was achieved it was decided in 1985 to supplement in-house development by the purchase of a commercially available system. The advantages of an effective

61. CAD-generated image of a cassette box allows study of detail before models are made, while images of a remote control unit compare different configurations, and final design of a television set checks conformity to components.

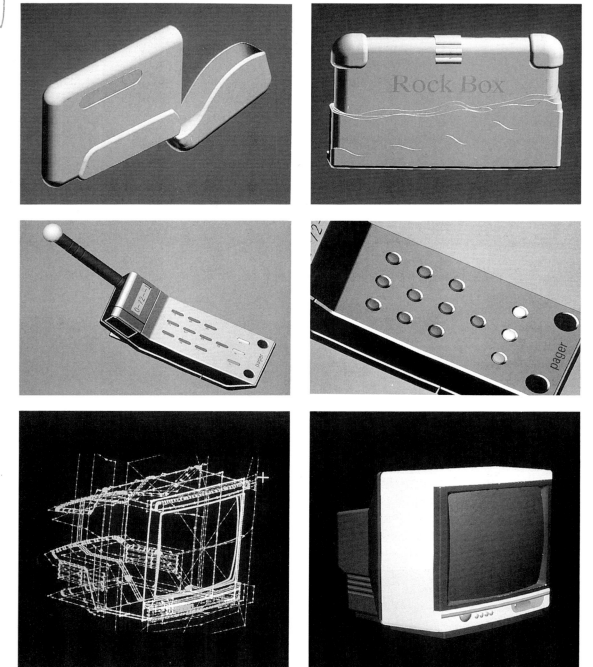

CAD system are, firstly, its capacity to partly replace physical models by computer models, which are available in greater range and variation; secondly, its ability to provide more specific means of evaluation, resulting in more effective design decisions at the start of the process, and thirdly, an exact definition of form, resulting in better communication and quality control (fig. 61). Since no specific industrial design oriented CAD system existed, the best available system capable of being customized was sought. It was installed in late 1986. The CAD studio within CID is responsible for systems management and together with the design teams, for implementing, by means of training and support, computer-aided design in the design process and the development in close cooperation with experts within and without the Philips organization, of CAD as a specific industrial design tool (fig. 62). For this close cooperation with the manufacturers of the commercial CAD system is considered essential.

A special training course for designers has been devised and by early 1988 fifteen product and graphic designers were following it. After a period of training designers can start a design project on the system. The full implementation of CAD in the design process, however, is still likely to take some time. Kees de Man, responsible for CID computer applications and systems development, has succinctly expressed the problem: 'As with all sophisticated technologies, the promise of the desired result often runs ahead of application realities.' To accelerate the application of CAD, consideration is being given to the creation of a group of 'superusers', consisting of trained designers from the design groups within CID.

The CID commitment is also being supplemented by projects in co-operation with the Technical University, Delft, and the Akademie voor Industriële Vormgeving, Eindhoven (AIVE). A start has been made in moving the CID training programme to AIVE, leaving the CAD studio free to develop practical applications.

New technical tools for design can result in new ways of seeing and expression, taking much of the repetitive drudgery out of design work. As

a working instrument, for example, CAD is capable of showing initial concepts, providing models for commissioners which can be consulted on the screen and varied to indicate the full range of possibilities (fig. 63). It can also be used as a control tool, for improved definition of formal qualities and communications in the total product development process. Once mat-

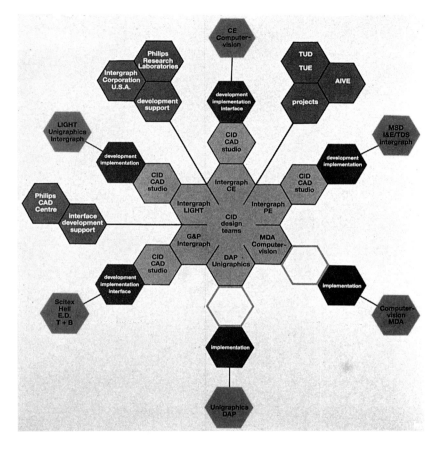

erial is specified on computer base it cannot be changed at any production point, anywhere in the world, without CID knowing. To use such new tools effectively means, however, that designers must respect them, and learn to adapt them to their skills, otherwise they could be made obsolete. 'That means going back to basics and learning how to do things well', says Blaich, 'we still need that hard, solid information level of basic design'.

The development of expertise in the field of ergonomics at Philips has an even longer background than CAD. Philips began investigating the potential of ergonomics in the early 1950s

62. Diagram of CAD in relationship to rest of Philips.

63. Example of CAD
diagram.

1987 two further staff were appointed.

One of McClelland's first tasks was the production of a Strategy Document. This was intended to provide a basis for action and generating
more awareness throughout the company of the
role of ergonomics in product design, not only in
designing the 'user interface', described as the
sum of those attributes of a product which a person must use to make the product work. The
document was also concerned with developing a
systematic methodology to demonstrate when an
interface is being accurately designed. Central
to this approach is the concept of 'usability'.
This can ensure that a product offers functions a
user wants, and that the functions can, via the
user interface, be used successfully. 'Usability
characteristics', the document states, 'can be
measured in terms of user efficiency and user
satisfaction. High levels of 'usability' also come
from products which are designed to be easy to
learn and to maintain.' This means moving from
the traditional 'remedial' role of the ergonomist
to making him an integral part of the product development team, able to anticipate problems
and ensure the inclusion of usability aspects
from the initial stages (fig. 64).

The drive to develop this fresh approach to
ergonomics and design was mainly stimulated
by the technology that Philips, among other corporations, was developing and thus the products
that CID was being required to design. By the
mid-1980s the move from 'hard' to 'soft' machines was emerging as a central change of emphasis for Philips as a whole and therefore also
for CID. The move was triggered by a decrease
in the costs of software technology, which stimulated interest in how this technology could be
used in product control systems. For the end-
user this often means more complexity, more
features to learn and more decisions to be made.
This had led in Philips, as in many companies,
to a greater emphasis on customer orientation in
design and marketing. To be acceptable by
users, the new 'soft' machines have to be easy to
learn, simple to use, and a more effective answer for a task (fig. 65).

There are few precedents for how this type of
design should be approached in practice, especially by a design group such as CID, so the

when the Institute for Perception Research
(IPO) was established as a joint activity between
Philips Research Laboratories and the Technical University in Eindhoven. Some of the work
of IPO was always concerned with incorporating
ergonomics into products of various types.

Besides these practical activities the Philips
Ergonomic Steering Committee was established. The committee is still active within
the company, organizing for and propagating
the importance of ergonomics. It now includes
representatives from, industrial design, research, IPO, industrial automation, occu-
pational health and several product divisions.
However in 1984 it was decided to establish an
applied ergonomics group within CID in order to
reinforce the existing ergonomics expertise
among design staff. Consequently Professor
Frank Leopold moved in September of that year
from IPO to CID, where he worked on stimulating the growth of this area until his retirement in
1986. He was succeeded as Manager, Applied
Ergonomics by Ian McClelland, who came from
the Institute for Consumer Ergonomics at
Loughborough University in England, where he
had built up considerable expertise in the application of ergonomics in many diverse areas. In

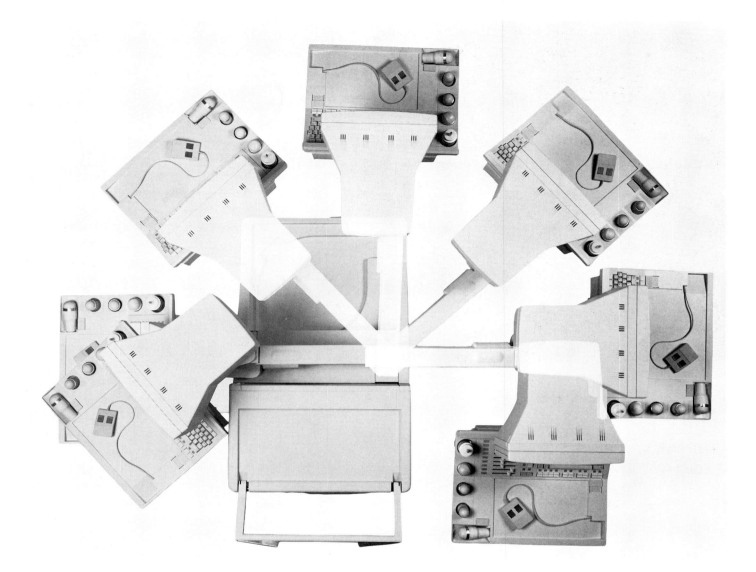

design of interfaces presents problems of both physical and psychological ergonomics. It was at this point that the definition of basic policy showed its value, for in approaching this problem several key concerns of established CID policy helped to lay guidelines for designing such an interface. These were set out in *inForm*, the CID journal, in 1986, which stated that any interface must be user-oriented; it is the capabilities of the user that are the limiting factors. Further, design proposals for the interface should be optimum. Press for the best. What was not possible this year may be next year. Designer should incorporate possibilities for test-

ing into design development, preferably with users, rather than leaving it until last. Designers should build on the principle of harmonization, and the possibility of family resemblance. Above all they must accept that this is a new field of design that cannot be taught, where experiment and learning from experience are needed before it can be said what resources are needed and how fast one can grow.

A further factor in the development of ergonomic expertise is the commercial pressure both to reduce development times and make the product development process more efficient, for example, in reducing the possibility of design

64. One of the studies for the Platinum project (product study page 124) shows ergonomic considerations used in the positioning of the monitor and console.

65. An example of the 'soft machine'.

error at all levels. This drive for product quality demands, however, accurate information about the market which can be incorporated into product specifications. Applied ergonomics has a particularly important contribution to make to product quality by specifying user requirements in products and in evaluating the effectiveness of design solutions. Potentially, however, the marketing philosophy of customer awareness can be given specific form within the whole product development process. It also means that a wider range of factors in product design can be clearly specified, and in many respects quantified, thus reducing the role of subjective opinion in decision-making.

Harmonization

The reorganization of CIDC in 1980-81 had as a primary aim, the establishment of closer working relationships with Product Divisions, assigning clear responsibilities for the achievement of this end. However, since the Philips organization is large, diverse and often dispersed, the working relations of the industrial design teams with the marketing and development experts of the Product Divisions had to take many forms. It was perhaps most easily achieved where all disciplines for a Product Division were located in one place. For example, personal care products such as shavers, hair-care, health and fitness products were concentrated at Drachten and domestic appliances at Groningen, both in The Netherlands, together forming the DAP. On each site an industrial design group could be concentrated to work with other disciplines, which encouraged engineers and marketing staff to regard them as integral members of divisional teams. Above all, close working contact on a day-to-day basis has enabled

the vitally important aspect of informal contact and understanding to develop. Peter Nagelkerke, describing the high level of co-operation in producing shavers at Drachten, tells of walks through the woods with colleagues from other disciplines in order to discuss problems, and comments: 'We all met in the bar and we all wanted to make the best shavers in the world!' A design centre has since been established at Groningen to serve the entire DAP range of activities. This was done to further integrate the designers into the marketing strategies of the product division and also create a single and strengthened design capacity. Complications occurred with the numerous international production centres and the few remaining national organization design groups, which frequently used specific technologies requiring a designer to be on hand. The sheer scale on which they were spread was in itself a problem. The centres where design staff were located spanned Australia, Austria, Belgium, Brazil, Canada, England, France, Germany, Hong Kong, Italy, India, Japan, Mexico, Singapore, Spain, Sweden and the USA.

However, the scale of complexity to be tackled if harmonization was to be a feasible policy went far beyond organizational or policy measures, and can be illustrated by the example of professional products. Five different Product Divisions manufactured equipment appropriate for use in a professional working context. These were: Electro-Acoustic (ELA), Data Systems (DS), Medical Systems Division (MSD), Science and Industry (S&I), and Telecommunication Systems (TS). Each developed their own product range according to their perception of the world market, without substantial reference to the others. The existing practice was for CID designers to work with commercial and technical staff, creating a market image for each division or even each product range. Furthermore, here too, products in each category were also occasionally developed by National Organizations for local needs, which competed with Concern products. The result was an uncoordinated design programme and multiplicity of design solutions. Yet equipment from different divisions frequently found application in the same environment, such as offices and medical laboratories, due, for example to the widespread introduction of data processing and miniaturized equipment housed in cabinets. The result was a confused visual identity across the whole spectrum of Philips professional products.

The nature of the problem was indicated in a report in the house journal in October, 1981, by Peter Doodson and Stefano Marzano, both of CID, following a visit to the SICOB exhibition in Paris, a major international trade fair for electronic equipment: 'Philips main stand was disappointing', they wrote, 'as it was in a flashy white and silver scheme and had no relation whatsoever to the Data Systems beige product colour schemes.' They continued, 'Although it might have been eye catching to the average visitor, it didn't help emphasize the unity we are striving for in the Data Systems product ranges. If anything, it emphasized the visual disunities that exist within our products and served to give

a clear crystallization of the problems that confront us as a company in trying to project a clear and coherent image to the public.' If such lack of co-ordination was evident in an exhibition stand, a relatively small scale, short term project completely within the control of the company, it was hardly surprising that more profound problems existed in the organization as a whole.

In 1984, during a further presentation to the annual joint meeting of the Philips Board of Management and heads of National Organizations at Ouchy in Switzerland, Robert Blaich considered the question of whether design operated as an integral part of corporate strategy. He was able to answer with a qualified 'yes'. In some areas co-operation was successfully contributing to corporate strategy — in others the potential of the contribution of industrial design was not fully perceived. Behind the qualified affirmative, however, lay a major investment of time and energy by CID in its commitment to the harmonization programme that was beginning to take effect.

In 1981 a functional harmonization programme commenced in co-operation between CID and the five product divisions concerned with professional products. The immediate goal was to relate the visual image of products directed to the same working environment, system or market group. This included such factors as the selection and design of colours and finishes, identification and product graphics, and product form. It was expected there would be further implications in terms of standardization programmes and internal economies. The long term policy implications were identified as concerned with international marketing requirements, with the differing range of product lifespans, and with Philips professional image — one that is contemporary, evolutionary, and has continuity. The immediate task of visual co-ordination was to be carried out on three levels, the corporate level, the level of application or environment (such as the product range) and thirdly at the level of the individual product or system (fig. 66).

The corporate level stressed a co-ordinated approach to readily definable factors, such as

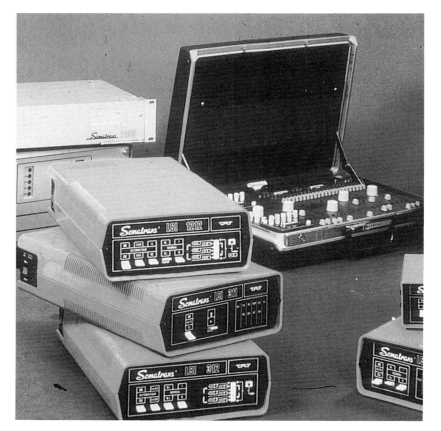

colour finish, product identification and Philips logo, graphics and formal characteristics, based on specifications in the corporate manual. For example, a suitable colour from the full harmonized range in the manual was selected for each professional product area. Work also commenced on specifying standardized textures and finishes, and standardized cabinets and work-stations, to be applied across Product Divisions.

Secondly, in a move away from a product-oriented design approach towards a user environment emphasis, specific rules and design guidelines were devised for situations where products from different Product Divisions met in particular fields of application, such as medical, business, and industrial environments. For example, in office environments, a range of products can be found, such as dictation systems and intercoms, through telecommunication equipment, word-processors and personal computers, to small business computers (fig. 67). Colour and logo-strips were the main

66. Test and measurement equipment before and after the professional harmonization programme redesign.

means used to create this relationship, using then existing specifications. However, this aspect of the programme has evolved to a point where a new specification has been produced, intended to give greater flexibility in the use of colours and graphics in the 1990s (fig. 68).

Finally, it was recognized that across a complex product range, many individual products or systems needed to be specifically designed for a particular purpose and market. In such cases, general stylistic criteria, taking account of the harmonization elements, but capable of adaptation over time, were considered more suitable than precise forms of standardization.

To further the professional harmonization programme, a Design Steering Committee was established, chaired by Robert Blaich, with representatives from the five Product Divisions, the Concern Standardization Department and CID, which reported to inter-Product Division management meetings. The re-organization of CID, with a team of designers working across a professional field, was obviously consistent

67. Desktop equipment – keyboards, dictation machines – before (above) and after harmonization (left).

68. Future harmonization plans shown in the projected Philips Home Interactive System.

with the emphasis on inter-Product Division design activities.

Further evidence of the drive for closer relationships across boundaries was provided by a move to co-ordinate audio and video activities, initially steered by Frans van der Put, the deputy head of CID, who was also acting as design manager for home entertainment/information equipment. An important factor influencing both audio and video equipment design was the spread of microchips, which replaced the integrated circuits dominant in electronics manufacture since the mid-1960s. On the basis of his experience as a contact designer for HiFi, Fons

Labohm wrote: 'A fact will be that the function will not determine the form but an acceptable form has to be created around parts that occupy very little space, very much challenging the slogan of the thirties, 'Form follows Function'' (fig. 69). The potential for miniaturization and co-ordination opened the way for audio and video equipment to be designed as components of a complete system, rather than separate products. Co-ordination between different areas was therefore not the only prerequisite for progress in this direction. As Labohm perceived, designers had to be prepared to radically change their approach.

The evidence they had done so, however, was provided by the Matchline concept which originated in CID and was developed with the Home Entertainment Systems group (HES). This is now in its third phase and brings HiFi and television/video equipment into a modular system which is technically integrated and visually coordinated, though all units can be bought separately. It saves space and duplication of components, ensures all units are compatible, and offers a unified remote control system, with the possibility of extension, including the addition of new technologies and uses as they come on line (fig. 70). It was slow moving when first introduced but is developing into a good market performer. Another modular system was designed by CID for Philips Home Interactive Systems (HIS) group. This combines audio, video, computer and optical technologies, and provides a high degree of information and interactivity. It also embodies possibilities for a high level of marketing flexibility with respect to specific applications, in the form of a comprehensive, and unique system(fig.68).

The Philips Kitchen Concept was an effort to integrate the range of small and major domestic appliances the corporation produced into new organization of kitchen functions. Major app-

69. Form no longer follows function, and allows a visual systems approach, as here in the Moving Sound range.

70. The current Matchline range (see also product study page 109)

liances were built in, storage for small appliances was provided, lighting and audio/visual aids were an integral element (fig. 71). Since Philips are not involved in the manufacture of kitchen units, the project was intended to stimulate kitchen manufacturers to look for and produce kitchens designed so that Philips products could be better integrated into the totality and consequently perform better. A further stage in this concept was a kitchen system specifically designed to meet the needs of elderly people.

The packaging harmonization for the Personal Care & Domestic Appliances division originated in a request from DAP in 1985 for an improved packaging image. The existing packaging was inconsistent and did not reflect the quality of product contained (fig. 72). After drawing up a brief, a small group of graphic designers selected nine products from across the DAP range to use as examples and worked through to the development of three-dimensional models. The final proposals were clear and consistent, combining the possibility of individual characteristics but within the overall identity. On acceptance of the packaging, a leaflet setting out the graphic guidelines of the concept was prepared by the DAP Harmonization Committee which includes CID

71. The Philips Kitchen concept.

members. In addition, the committee regularly evaluates the programme, and its permission must be obtained before any deviation from the established guidelines is introduced, as in extending the concept of white background for white/grey products to allow a black background for products of that colour, for example, hairdryers for men and travel clocks (fig. 73).

By 1986 the harmonization programme for Professional Products was yielding substantial results. An example was the programme to develop a unified visual image for the entire product range of the Philips Medical Systems, which presented particular problems. Market

requirements had to be considered, as in any sector of production, but medical equipment is applied in environments and with particular user needs, both in terms of medical staff and patients, which impose stringent responsibilities on designers and manufacturers. The programme provided a coherent visual image by implementing a standard colour and logostrip, with unnecessary details being eliminated to maximize product simplicity. The overall aim, however, progressed far beyond visual co-ordination, to the intention of developing a total range of products in which qualities of function, construction and durability could be implicitly

72. Packaging for small domestic appliances before and after redesign.

relied upon, and which by quality of design would enhance the patient-practitioner relationship. A crucial feature for both sides of that relationship was the need for excellence in ergonomic design, attempting both to mitigate the apprehension of patients, whilst providing ease and simplicity of control by practitioners, thus helping create an atmosphere of confidence. This could only be achieved if design staff were involved in a project from the earliest development stages. In this respect, the Platinum Project for an ultra-sound scanner is an excellent example of potential realized (fig. 74).

Another outstanding example of the development of harmonization policy was launched at the 1986 Hanover Fair. The Philips Electronic Office System (PEOS) was designed under the

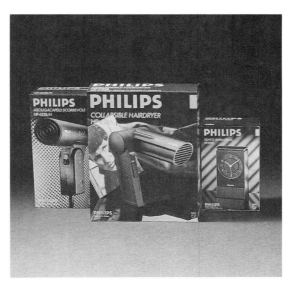

73. New developments in packaging.

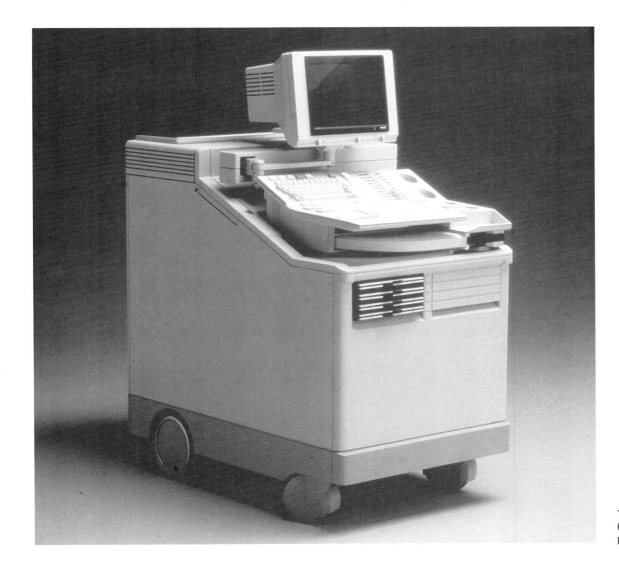

74. The Platinum project (see also product study page 125)

75. The Philips Electronic Office System (see also product study pages 119-123).

direction of Robert Blaich, whose experience in the commercial and office furniture and equipment industry prior to joining Philips convinced him of a lack of adequate furniture systems that were fully compatible with automated equipment. An obvious extension of Philips involvement in automated office equipment, he felt, should be to provide support structures of this kind (fig. 75). 'I prefer to think of the office system we have designed as a support system rather than furniture. Furniture has traditionally had a life of its own, and while office furniture has in recent years been more concerned with responding to human needs with ergonomic design solutions, it is quite new to think additionally in terms of responding to equipment demands. And so, with automated equipment dominating the office, furniture becomes subordinated to the equipment, or is, in fact, really a support for the equipment. I saw such a system as an unsolved need in the marketplace.' From the beginning of the project it was con-

ceived as part of the Professional Products Harmonization programme, and it marked an important step forward from the level of coordination of existing equipment to the level of innovation in product development across the boundaries (fig. 76).

As in other areas of Philips design management, these developments were accompanied by a definition of policy, in part emerging from practice, in part intended to shape it in new directions. Two volumes of a Harmonization Manual for Philips Professional Products had been prepared by 1986. Volume 1 concentrated mainly on setting out design guidelines and policy for product harmonization and requirements for packaging graphics, and was generally intended for those responsible for the definition, management, presentation and promotion of Philips professional products. The material covered 'Common Characteristics', such as logostrips, colour and graphics, which were applicable to all professional products, and 'Typical Characteristics', applicable to products used in the same environment, such as, medical, office or laboratory environments. Volume II was predominantly concerned with mechanical and industrial design, manufacturing, quality control and purchasing. It consisted of standardization specifications on requirements, preferred materials, working instructions and test methods. A loose-leaf format was chosen to allow constant up-dating and extension. For example, further work on Volume 1 was directed towards establishing guidelines for the harmonization of product presentation at fairs and exhibitions, and in brochures and other publications. The format also enabled, where appropriate, the insertion of local Product Division standards and instructions.

'Harmonization is a word I use when putting people together.' says Robert Blaich. 'See if they have something in common, begin with agreement rather than with rules, and the standards will emerge later.' Viewed in that perspective, harmonization does not have to imply rigidity. In generating this idea, CID has made a profoundly significant contribution not just to design in Philips, but to the whole concept of corporate management.

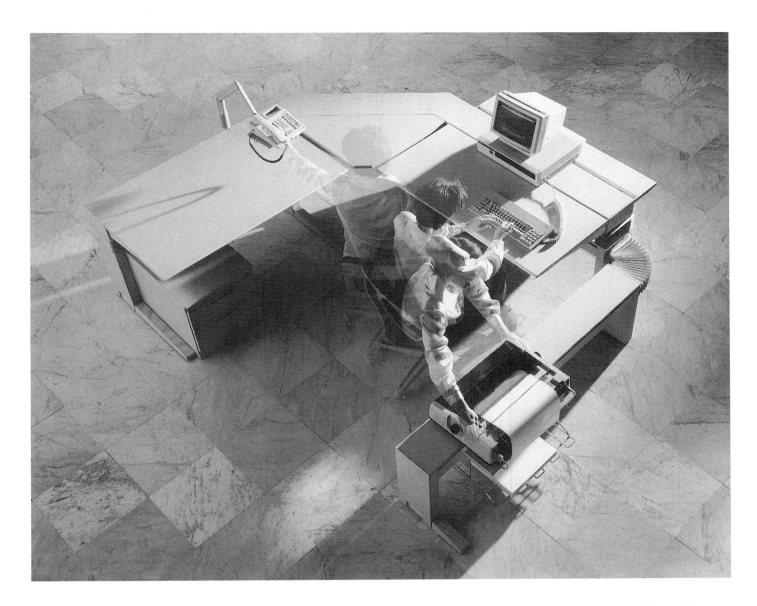

Communications

In a paper published in 1986, Robert Blaich wrote '. . . most of all, design management is about selling the design necessity to your own corporation or clients on a continuous, day-by-day basis. Anyone not willing to be a salesperson for design need not apply for the design manager job'.

In creating an organizational structure and policies clearly indicating the new paths CID would have to follow, formal points of reference were established which identified aims, roles and responsibilities. These were a necessary framework, the bones of the process of re-organization. However, for the new structure to become a living organism, in other words, to have a sense of purpose and vitality, an understanding of the role of CID and close identification with it by all its staff is also of paramount importance. Since his arrival at Philips, Robert Blaich has devoted considerable effort to ensuring his staff are consulted and kept informed on developments affecting CID, its work and achievements. Moreover, if design is to function effectively within any organization, especially one as large and complex as Philips, then clear communication of values and objectives with all

76. PEOS as part of a complete system: a study used to demonstrate the ergonomic efficiency of the workstation.

71

levels of management on a regular, on-going basis becomes an absolute necessity. Finally, if a company's efforts to achieve a reputation for design quality are to be adequately recognized, then it also has to communicate its values to a wider audience outside.

As part of the process of informing staff of significant developments both within the company and without, what at CID is called the Service Center plays a vitally important role. It contains a variety of resources. The book stock includes standard works and manuals covering the fields of technology, design technique, theory and history, supported by a comprehensive selection of international design and technical journals and catalogues, and brochures from current exhibitions. Information about future exhibitions and design events is also compiled and circulated. Reports and material collected by staff visiting exhibitions is collected and circulated to all for whom it is relevant. There are files containing data on the market range of all products and processes with the remit of CIDC, supported by an extensive slide library constantly extended in coverage. All Philips publications are naturally included, but other documentation includes consumer reports, data on new materials, techniques and innovations of general relevance. The Service Center not only responds to specific requests from designers in relation to work in hand, but recognizing the inevitable problems of keeping abreast of a huge range of literature, it sends relevant copies of important material to people working in particular fields.

A major instrument of communication for designers and throughout the company is the CID news-sheet inForm. This was redesigned in 1981 and transformed from a small-size, visually dull pamphlet to a colourful, well-illustrated newspaper, regularly published four times a year (fig. 77). It is produced by a team within CID with a professional editor as consultant and contains articles on matters affecting design work or major developments and achievements, regular reports from staff in all sectors of CID and news of personnel. A regular column by Robert Blaich provides a flow of ideas, comment and exhortation. inForm is a valuable means of keeping design staff across the world aware of developments and ideas, and it is also a useful means of information amongst the commissioners of CID, being sent to over a thousand managers within Philips.

Communication with management at all levels is a major priority for Robert Blaich and all the Design Managers. At the highest level, **an annual meeting with the Group Management Committee is the occasion for a review of achievements, performance and for presentations of** future plans. Regular presentations to management meetings at various levels are a means of presenting the broad strategic issues affecting the work of CID, supported by pamphlets, brochures and other publications which diffuse information about CID throughout the Philips organization. Visits to the CID complex by groups such as the Product Division Management Groups enable colleagues to see and experience for themselves something of the atmosphere surrounding the design function, by touring the studios and talking to designers at their drawing-boards about work in progress. Again, discussions and evaluation sessions on the role of design are an integral part of such visits. Such occasions provide valuable opportunities for interchange between the various levels of responsibility, and one of a number of practices and procedures to ensure that ideas and policies would not simply flow in a 'top down' direction.

In May, 1985, in an effort to stimulate a

77. inForm: cover of the 25th issue.

better working relationship with Marketing and Product Development/Production managers, CID organized a two-day seminar on design management. Using outside experts on the subject as well as senior Philips management, seventy-five staff participated, twenty-five each from industrial design, marketing and product development. They were divided into working groups to consider topics such as long-term strategic planning, product planning and innovation, amongst many others, with groups reporting back with their recommendations. It was an experiment to see what they had in common. 'Everybody agreed we had to work together and more coherently', said Robert Blaich, delighted at its success, 'It was a key moment when we started to understand the need to integrate.' It also encouraged a decisive change of approach, away from arbitrary and subjective values, to an understanding and implementation of defined criteria that can be discussed, agreed and understood, not only by designers but by anyone involved in a project. In practice, this change of role has been realized to a considerable extent in the harmonization programme, but the seminar stimulated genuine understanding at a decisive level of management.

78. Design for Market logo.

The potential of the approach adopted in the seminar was demonstrated when one of the recommendations which emerged from it was taken up by the Corporate Organization and Efficiency Department, with representatives from Product Divisions and CID acting in an advisory role. This was for a co-ordinate approach to product renewal and was put into effect under the title 'Design for Market' (fig. 78). This emphasized the need for management in all mainline functions to co-operate and integrate efforts in the product renewal process. Participants from business units, design, development, production and marketing use a variety of approaches and case studies in joint sessions, drawing on techniques developed in their own area of expertise, and also that of expert advisors. The 'Design for Market' programme is on-going, with for example, a workshop in May, 1987, featuring renewal proposals for in-car entertainment, rotashavers and dish-washers.

The purpose of much of the flow of information from CID within the company is, of course, to persuade as many people in the organization as possible of the importance of design. Whilst Robert Blaich is adamant on the subject of the importance of design as a competitive tool in the corporate strategy, he recognizes that the task of persuading colleagues of this is a continuous and on-going one. Design consciousness must permeate all levels of the corporate consciousness and particularly that of management decisions. With changes in design technology, such as the availability of computer software enabling many design functions to be carried out by staff without design training, Blaich believes many traditional roles and techniques of today's designers could become rapidly outmoded, with a corresponding need for them to increasingly switch to design management, in order to maintain standards.

Creating an awareness of Philips commitment to design and quality in the design community and with the general public is also a regular feature of the activities of CID. Again it can take many forms, from the high academic to straight publicity. As an example of the former, Blaich, van der Put, and other CID staff are regular contributors to conferences, design com-

79. The jury for Neste's annual technology awards: (left to right) Antti Nurmesniemi, Jaakko Ihamuotila (President of Neste), Robert Blaich, Mario Bellini and Kenji Ekuan.

80. The racing yacht 'Philips Innovator' and some of the ancillary designs.

petition juries and publications (fig. 79), explaining their ideas and practices, often making significant contributions to the theory of design and its management. In 1987, for example, Robert Blaich is President of ICSID, and he is playing a major role in the World Design Expo conference in Nagoya, Japan, in 1989. In comparison, the sponsorship by the company of the **racing** yacht, the *Philips Innovator* for the Whitbread Round-the-World race of 1984 (in which it was runner-up) was an opportunity for CID to undertake a total design approach to every aspect of the boat, its crew equipment and the associated publicity (fig. 80). CID have also sponsored and contributed to exhibitions for the general public in many countries.

Design competitions are a means of setting Philips products against their competitors under the scrutiny of independent judges. In 1987, 62 awards were received, including some of the most prestigious in the field, such as the ID Design Review in the USA, where the Expressobar coffeemaker was a winner in the consumer product category (fig. 81). The Japanese 'G' Mark was awarded to five items, and the Gute Industrieform in West Germany to no less than thirty-one. There were also awards from the Dutch Design Council and the Austrian Design Institute. Seven new products were also added to the permanent collection of Die Neue Sammlung, Munich, the West German museum of applied art. The record of such success in recent years is becoming impressive (fig. 82, 83)

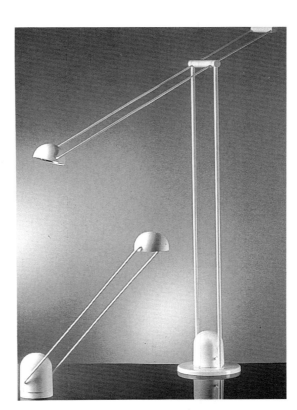

81. The Expressobar coffeemaker, winner of a 1987 ID Design Award (see also product study page 93)

82. Lamp that won a Gute Industrieform prize in 1987.

83. The Philips CD player, an early model, now in the collection of the Museum of Modern Art, New York.

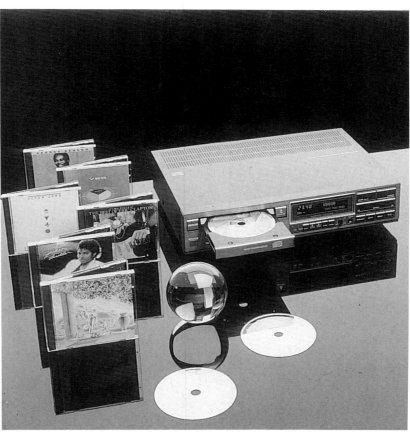

Towards Total Quality

Everyone involved with the management of design in CID freely admits there are still products and areas of activity which need improvement. Nevertheless, the influence of design is spreading throughout the organization and focussing on the question of how to improve quality. 'I would state that a product or product system is of total quality,' says Frans van der Put, 'when the experience of users with respect to all functional aspects are in harmony with their expectations. This experience will result in confidence in the product and consequently confidence in the manufacturer of same.' It is a statement of an ideal, but vision is necessary to give a sense of purpose. On the subject of moving closer to the ideal, Robert Blaich says, 'In some cases I've seen a hundred percent improvement, in some cases I've seen very little, in most cases its gone up and on average I'd say we are about eighty per cent of the way there. I still see

room for improvement but in some cases I'm proud. And that for me is a sign that things are happening.' In any large manufacturing organization there is inevitably a tension between the demands for quantity and quality, between getting into a market and getting it right. The two need not conflict, but building a sense of quality across such a large product range takes time, it is an incremental process, difficult to construct, fragile and constantly needing attention, and easily destroyed.

Perhaps the final comment on what is being achieved in design at Philips as a result of able and intelligent management can be left to someone outside CID. In September, 1986, **Robert Riphagen, then the company's Director of Corporate Advertising** wrote: 'We don't hide the product any more . . . The product has become the hero of our ads'.

84. The CID headquarters building in Eindhoven.

PRODUCT STUDIES

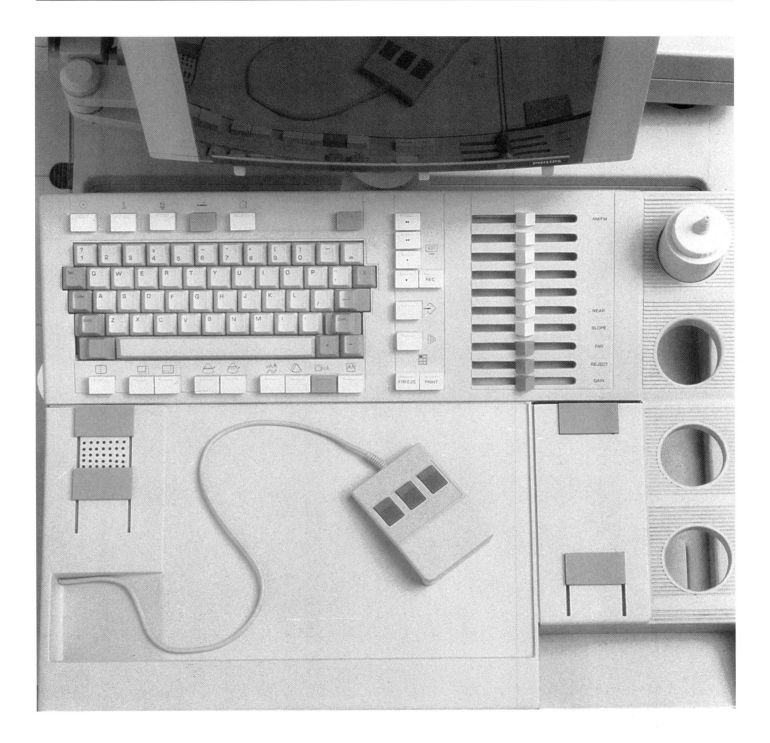

The Philishave Tracer

The Philips 'Philishave' dry shavers have been on the market since before the Second World War, the range growing from a shaver with a single shaving head to the present selection of two and three head razors. Two-headers have been in the programme since the 1950s and in that sense the Tracer, as a two-header, is not really exceptional. However, it is interesting because of the total approach involved in its development, with contributions from marketing research, product management, application, manufacturing, distribution, advertising and promotion, as well as CID.

It is estimated that throughout the world, more than half of the men who shave use a razor blade. Outside Europe, the number of blade users is larger than the number of electric shaver users, whereas in Europe electric and blade shaving are on average more in balance. In Europe, some nine million electric shavers are sold each year and Philips is the market leader. In such a highly competitive situation growth is unlikely to come from increasing market share at the expense of competitors. It is necessary to look to enlarging the size of the market. Two factors could detrimentally affect the European dry shaver market: firstly, an increase in the economic lifetime of electric shavers, leading to existing models being kept in use longer; or, secondly, an increase in wet shaving.

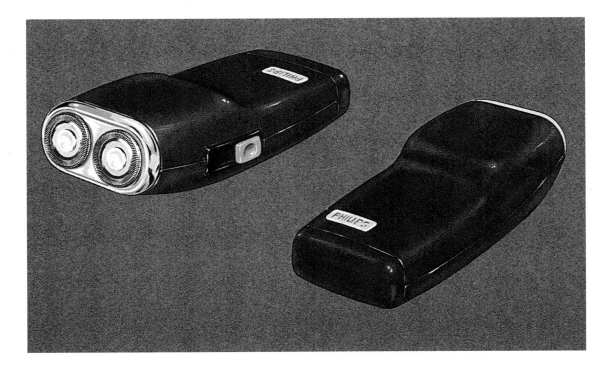

85. Study models for the original Tracer range.

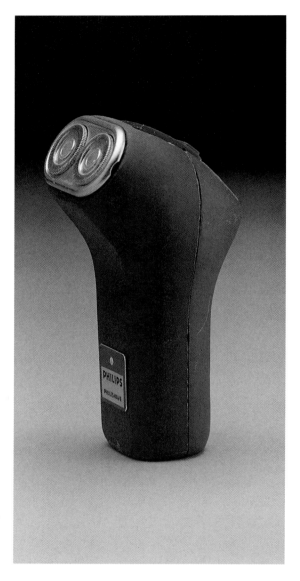

85. Study models for the original Tracer range.

The first is a replacement problem. This can be affected by a lack of perceived product innovation, or satisfaction with the current shaver, or a decline in disposable income. The second is in essence an initial market problem. Research shows that the initial choice of shaving habit by young men generally determines their system choice for the rest of their life. A reduction in blade shaving costs, or a lack of product or of packaging appeal in electric shavers for the 15-24 age group, could lead to an eventual decline in electric shaving. The differences between these two major market segments are therefore significant and individual marketing strategies are required for the replacement and for the initial market. Philips concluded that thelatter — the initial youth market — had received insufficeint attention and a new initiative was needed.

In the early 1980s the Philips shaver range showed an increasingly modern look with a strong emphasis on technical image and communication of new features, such as adjust-

ability and lift blade systems. Advertising was used to support these characteristics. The policy of Philips is that each Philishave Electric Shaver should have an improvement in shaving performance over its predecessor, evidenced by features which can be communicated to the customer. The target market was therefore existing dry shaver users. No real youth oriented shaver was on the market.

The origins of the Tracer programme resulted from an interesting set of coincidences. Around the same time in the early 1980s, CID design groups in the Netherlands and in Japan were asked to do form studies on two-headed razors (fig. 85). In Japan this initiative was intended for the local market with its different functional requirements, and in the Netherlands as successors to a then existing range in the lower segment of the market; the national organization in Australia wanted to position a two-header at a lower price level under the name of Philishave Tracer; and the 'Youth Task Force' was established to make proposals for a youth approach in Philips products.

This led in 1983 to a definition of marketing objectives to increase Philishave sales in the 15-19 age group by introducing a Philishave specially designed for the youth target group, choosing price points to suit the purchasing power of the youth target group, adapting dis-

tribution and visibility at point of purchase, and creating a product image appealing to the target group. The strategy for the initial market approach was therefore worked out in terms of product, price, promotion and distribution as a total marketing strategy. As to the product itself, the product mix concept included the technical specification, and design elements, such as texture, decorative features, colour, product graphics, packaging for use, display packaging and brand name.

The product was specified in a mains and rechargeable version (fig. 86). The mains version was intended to hit the lower price point and the rechargeable to fit closely the target group with its image of portability and convenience. For reasons of compactness the two-header concept was preferred instead of the three header, des-

86. Original Tracer range showing alternative versions.

88. The original Tracer and soft wallet.

87. The two original colour ranges and their separate but related advertising, aimed at the youth market.

pite some initial concern at the two-header gaining market share from the larger shaver. The product, it was further specified, should have a good performance for the primary functions of shaving and trimming, and the mains version should have a dual voltage switch for 110 and 220 volts. The rechargeable model should have a built-in charger and universal voltage. The target group, not being homogeneous, should have a choice in colour versions also. On the basis of market tests four colours were selected: black and red for the mains version, blue and silver for the rechargeable (fig. 87). A special soft wallet was designed to support the youth image of sports and fashion (fig. 88), which was extended to link with the so-called 'helmet sports'. This sporty image was communicated through the packaging design and promotional material. The self-standing image of the youth shaver was strengthened through the brand-name Tracer, which led to the fast creation of a different image, in support of the segmentation concept.

Image tests showed that the Tracer was very

THE LOOKS OF A WINNER

89. Tracer I with dynamic sports association.

positively perceived by youngsters as more modern, young, attractive, advanced, but still having a good shaving performance even when compared to the Philishave three-header. Research was also done on the level of price-setting through market tests. Innovation in the area of distribution lay in the attempt to create a direct association between Tracer and fashion and other high interest products for youngsters. The use of barbers' shops as communication channels was supplemented by selling through audio/video outlets and also through supermarkets in a special blister packaging.

The advertising objectives were the creation of awareness and preference for Philishave Tracer with the target group and an increase of interest and acceptance of the electric shaving system. The target group for the advertisements were the potential users (young men of 15-24 years of age), potential gift buyers, and the trade. The advertising position was 'Philishave Tracer: the young, dynamic way to shave' and advertisements were intended to radiate an atmosphere which fitted a youngster's world and lifestyle. The creative execution associated Philishave Tracer with the winners in the world of dynamic sports, a recognizable and credible world for the target group. As communication colour, red was used, a choice intended to be dominant, eye-catching, aggressive and dynamic (fig. 89).

The results of introducing the Tracer onto the market proved most successful. The goal to attract young men for the Philishave rotary system was reached and the age profile of the Tracer users proven to be correct. It was also clear that many youngsters were now new Philishave Electric Shaver users.

Based on the success of the Philishave Tracer, in 1987 the new programme was introduced based upon the same starting points. The design

90. The Tracer II product range.

execution in form and colour shows a somewhat more aggressive and technical approach. Within given ergonomic tolerances a more faceted and dramatic basic design was made and the colour setting was done in primary colours and black (fig. 90). To achieve higher contrasts (and so more drama) the construction was changed from two house halves into two housing parts with side panels. Every functional part of the shaver are made recognizable either by form or by colour while product graphics indicate clearly what the features of the product are, so the difference between rechargeable and mains versions is recognizable at first glance. The background colour of dark grey was chosen to set off these more sparkling colours. Again the

91. Tracer II display packaging, using blister packs.

colour red, the Tracer logo and the link to helmet sports are the vehicles for the Tracer image (fig. 91). The programme continues to be highly successful. Andre Rotte, appointed design manager for Personal Care Products in 1986 found on his arrival that the design of the new Tracer range was in hand and market testing of the colour scheme and graphics was in progress: 'in studying the Tracer case I was impressed and enthused by the high consistency of the approach to this particular target group and of the product and design execution.' The development of the first and second Tracer shavers demonstrates the potential of innovative marketing and design concepts being worked out from the earliest stages on a co-operative basis between the different disciplines involved.

I The Tracer shaver has been extremely successful in introducing electric shaving to a new and younger clientele: it has also played an important role in bringing the Philips name before the youth market.

II A Philips poster from the 1930s, designed by Louis Kalff. It stresses the product, though other posters of the time (see p.10) used more conventional themes.

III The first Philips CD player. As with audio cassettes, Philips' development of the compact disc became the industry standard.

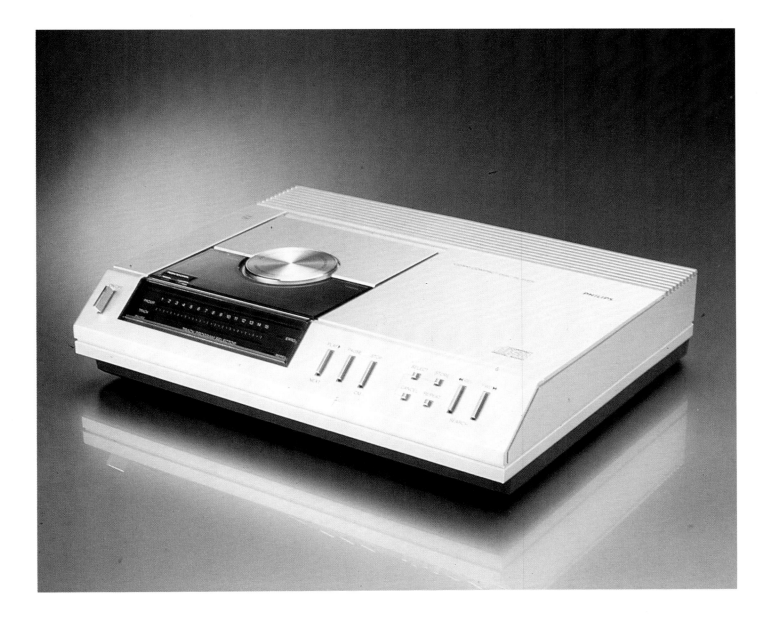

IV The new range of Philips Vacuum Cleaners. The development of this range is discussed in the product study on page 146.

V Harmonization policies (p.60) are particularly important in relation to
packaging, seen here in audio-visual products.

VI, VII Two major new professional products are the Professional Video
Camera (see product study p.130) and the Platinum ultrasound scanner
(see product study p.124). The Platinum has just been awarded a Gute
Industrieform prize for outstanding design.

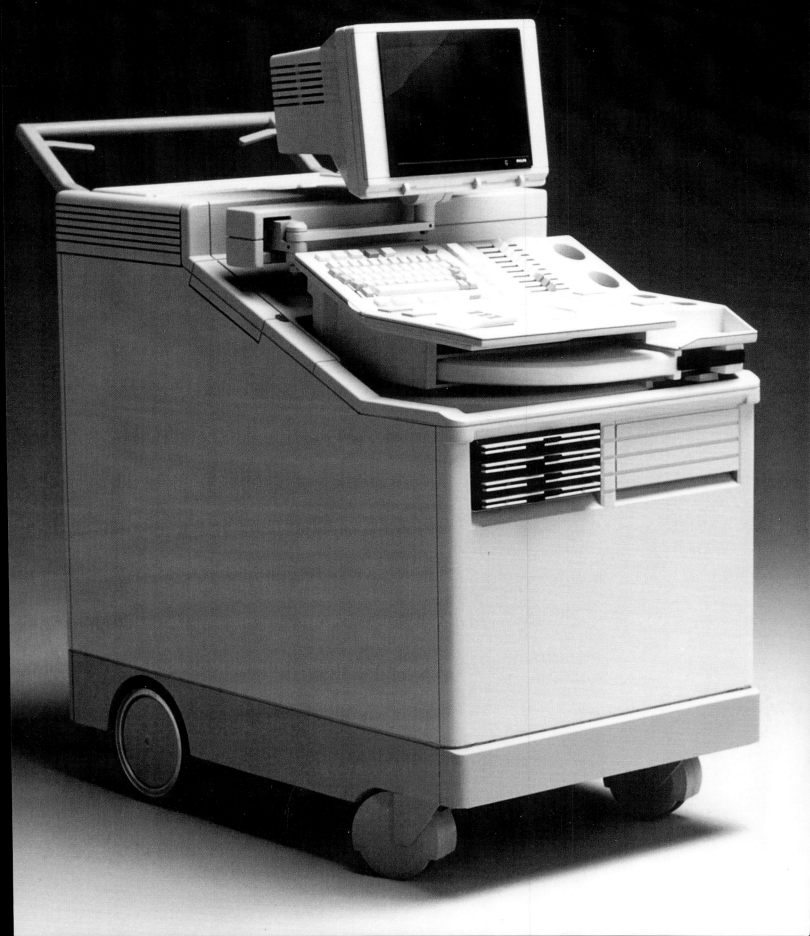

Coffee makers

The first Philips coffee maker, the 'Coffee Cona' was produced in 1964 and by the 1970s a wide range of coffee makers had been successfully introduced into markets across the world. Philips, for example, were the first company successfully to introduce coffee machines into Japan, traditionally a tea drinking country. By 1980, however, the market for such appliances was reaching saturation point, and with increasing competition, prices were subjected to ever greater pressure. Therefore in the early 1980s Philips product policy with regard to coffee makers was redefined as a broad basic programme that allowed for both differentiation and global design. In short, Philips world-wide presence and good sales organization in many countries calls for broad mass-oriented, mass-producible product ranges, for, with economies of scale, it is possible for Philips to remain competitive in the coffee maker market. But in addition to the mass global market there is also a growing demand for differentiation in various segments of the market, resulting from different lifestyles, both between and within cultural groups, as well as from changes in family structure, and from differing functional needs. In order to meet both these aspects of demand, the design of appliances had to be not only suitable for mass-production but capable of appealing to market segments across the world.

On this basis of this product policy, work began to upgrade the existing range of coffee makers (fig. 92) with a coherent range of new, modern coffee makers. This was directed by Lou Beeren, who during this period was responsible for the design activities of Kitchen Appliances. The new range evolved through a programme-oriented approach involving a product creation team composed of representatives from marketing, technical development, manufacturing and industrial design. Within the team, each function had equal status. In the past industrial designers had a subordinate status in this area of product development, being restricted to giving advice and providing services. The new equal status was therefore an **important step forward. In part it was** due to a recognition of the change in market conditions. With the increase in competition, it became clear that the range of products on offer from other manufacturers were to the consumer virtually equivalent in economic and technical

92. The range of coffee makers before redesign.

VIII Research into new forms for Coffee Makers led to this innovative design for an After Dinner Coffee machine.

terms. There was therefore a shift from the hardware aspects of the product to software aspects, in which use factors and visual qualities play a leading role. The success of this policy has resulted in Philips becoming market leaders world-wide in the field of coffee makers.

The Product Range

Café Duo

The Café Duo already existed as a successful model, a simple one and two cup coffee maker that was a real global product, selling well in all parts of the world (fig. 93). It was believed by the product creation team that a good, strong product should not be unnecessarily changed, but should rather mature. The model introduced in 1984 was therefore an improved product, maintaining the basic characteristics of the old, but with enhanced polypropylene material for the housing and refinements in the form, the availability of different kinds of filters, and the option of a wall-mounting (fig. 94) Sales increased dramatically, to the point where production could not keep pace with demand.

93. Existing Café Duo model.

94. Two foam study models for the Cafe Duo design, and the redesigned version in the middle.

Café Duo Select

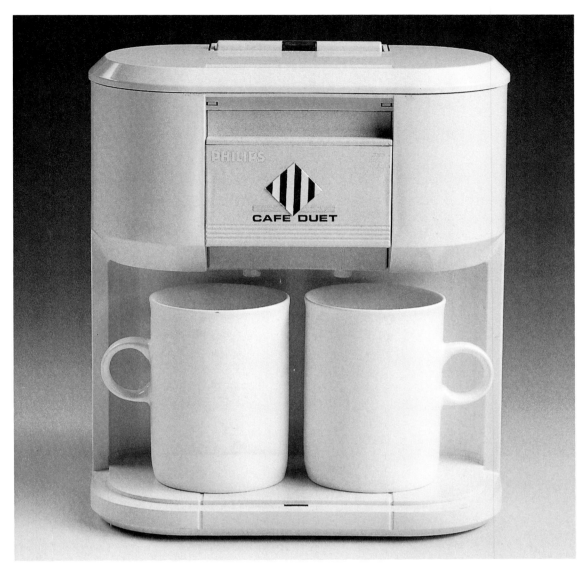

95. A special version of Café Duo as a youth product.

Development and design are an ongoing process, and the introduction of a new product is the start of the development of its successor (fig. 95). The life cycles of consumer products are becoming shorter, and to avoid superficial styling changes as a short term measure for differentiation it is necessary that constant analyses be made, based on feedback from the market, information vital to improve both production and application. In order to maintain Philips success in this market, the Café Duo Select (fig. 96) was introduced in 1987. It is designéd so that the power unit, which includes the pump and all electric parts, can be disconnected, making it possible to take the front housing to a dishwasher or a sink for cleaning.

96. The Café Duo Select.

Café Lait

This is a clear target-group product. In many countries it is habitual to add milk to coffee, but adding cold milk can affect the taste of the coffee by considerably reducing its temperature. The solution is to use warm milk, but this requires further utensils and constant attention, for to boil milk affects its taste, and for milk to boil over creates considerable cleaning problems. **The Café Lait is a unique product which, among a range of features, will heat milk to seventy-five degrees centigrade while brewing coffee (fig. 97).**

97. The Café Lait.

Café Therm

Standard coffee makers keep coffee hot with a warming plate. Although this feature is appreciated by the consumer, the process of keeping the coffee hot can affect its taste. A coffee maker with an isolated jug for the hot coffee therefore has some major advantages, in that the taste of the coffee is kept intact, while the jug can be removed from the coffee maker once coffee is brewed, freeing the appliance from the kitchen and letting it be used for example in the garden or at the dinner table. In addition, research had shown that 'jug independence' was very important for coffee makers in small businesses, where it reduced the interruption involved in obtaining a cup of coffee.

In 1982 an existing standard coffee maker

was adapted for use with a thermos jug, which was comparable to the competition. Working from this experience, however, the product creation team believed they could make a superior product. The result was the HD of 1986 (fig. 98). The jug was developed in close cooperation with the Thermos company, with a small exposed surface for the liquid, for example, to reduce the risk of the coffee deteriorating through air contact. A double walled glass jug also proved to have better thermal qualities and to be more resistant to breakage. To integrate the jug into the housing required that it had no protruding spout, however, and the design of a flush, no-dribble spout required considerable research and numerous test models before a satisfactory solution was

achieved. The jug has in addition a protective ring at its base to absorb shock when it is put down. Other features include automatic switch-off after brewing (there is no hot plate) and the choice of free-standing or wall mounted use. The watertank is detachable, and has small ribs for easier handling and measures for eight to ten cups. Cord storage at the back retains excess cord length.

When the first dummy of this model was presented in 1983, there was some marketing feeling that the product was too clean and too advanced for the market, until a consumer test showed a very favourable score for the new design. It has since won a series of major design awards and has been very successful in the market.

98. The Café Therm: note the lipless jug.

Café Royal

Another addition to the series is the Café Royal range which comprises five models of various sizes and includes additional features, such as a freshness indicator and a clock and timer (fig. 99). The range is intended for a broad medium and high end segment of the European market, with a clean form composed of geometric elements and a swing filter that has a simple hinge solution for easy handling. Other features are a water level indicator, automatic switch-off after two hours, and cord storage.

99. Models for the Café Royal.

The Expresso Duo and the Expressobar

100. The Espresso Duo.

These products are also aimed at specific market segments. The Duo is a compact espresso maker for one or two cups with a steam pipe for frothing and heating milk for cappucino (fig. 100). The Espresso Bar is a top of the range model with all features necessary to make a professional cup of espresso (fig. 101).

Future developments may incorporate some re-evaluation of the ritual aspects of coffee drinking by bringing coffee making to the dinner table: The Café Gourmet (fig. 102) is a design initiative by Lou Beeren to illustrate new possibilities for electric coffee making, a trend also suggested in the After Dinner Coffee Maker (fig. 103), a student project by Saskia Din-

100. First model for the Expressobar.

101. The Expressobar final model with packaging.

gelstad's from the Technical University of Delft, developed in close co-operation with CID. Leisure, sociability and technology come together in the making and drinking of coffee, and through exploring this conjunction Philips intend to remain major producers in this market.

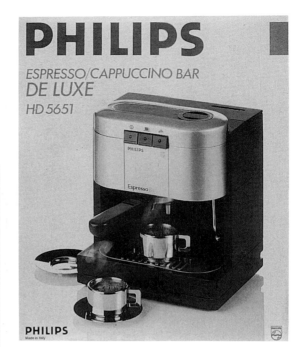

102. Café Gourmet, a proposed 'dinner table top' coffee maker.

103. After Dinner Coffee, a student project during a study visit to CID.

IX A recent Philips seminar looked at product semantics (p.56). This
"Beethoven Radio" was one product concept to be developed during the
seminar.

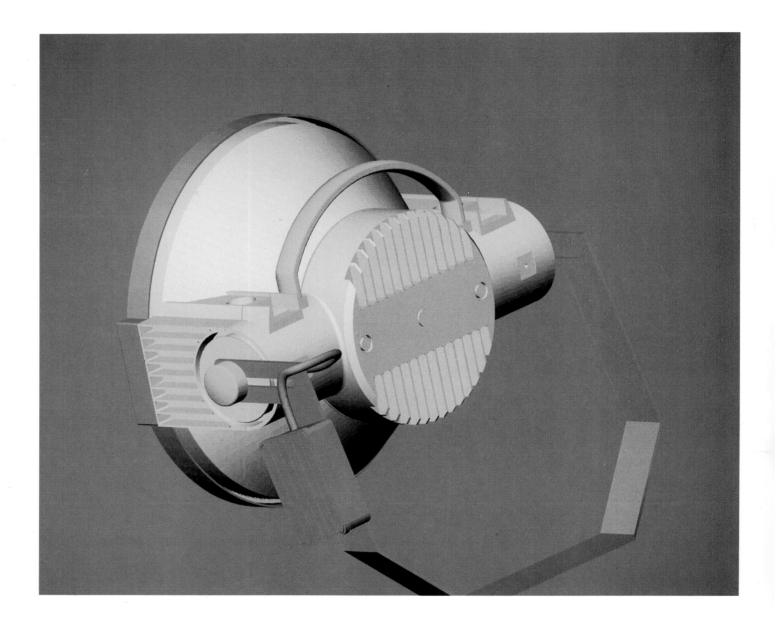

X The Arena Vision Sportslight (product study p. 141) was developed
through extensive use of CAD (Computer Aided Design).

XI One future development in lighting, a classic area of Philips activity, is
this project for a tracked spotlight.

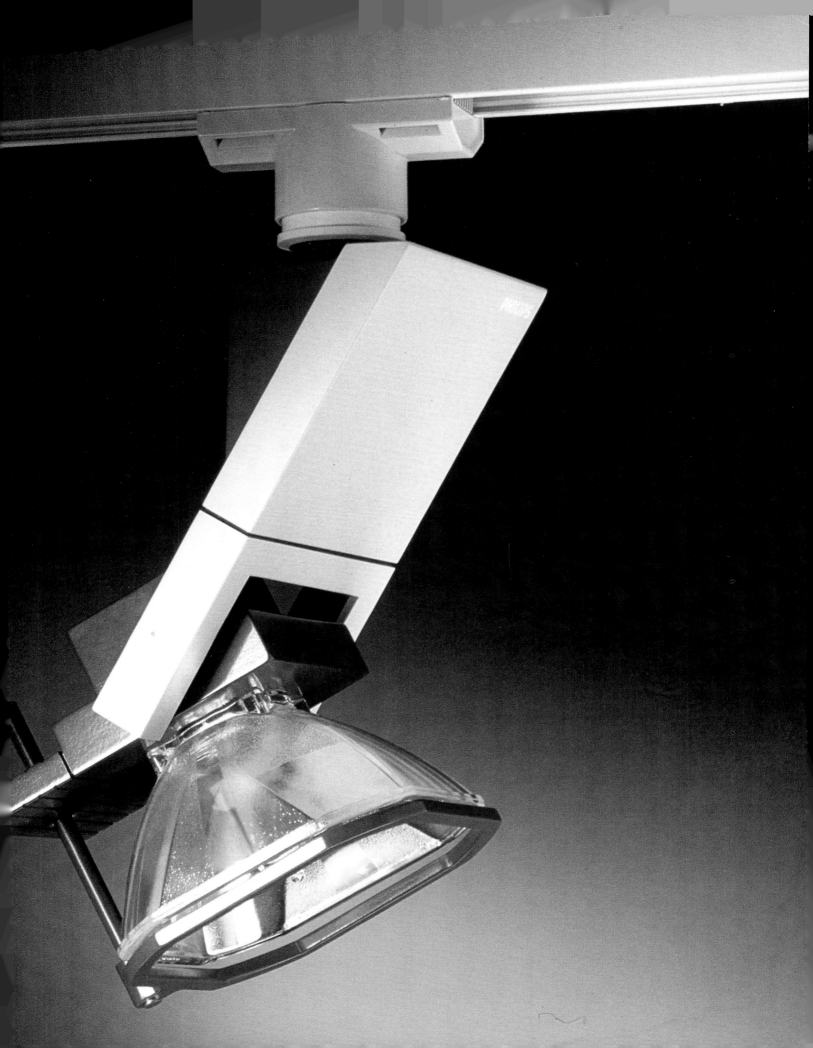

XII, XIII The Roller Radio is a design-led venture (see product study
p.135), and has led to other design concepts such as the "Wave Radio"
(right).

XIV, XV, XVI The Philips Electronic Office System was devised to meet
the needs of the modern office (see p. 119): the Home Interactive System
(above) is a project to bring information and entertainment systems of all
kinds into the home in a unified way. The Matchline System (overleaf)
already achieves this with a modular design for entertainment systems.

Matchline

The concept of this system illustrates the role CID has come to play in leading developments within Philips. In 1981, anticipating the possibility of combining audio and video units together, CID initiated a design study into this subject, resulting in the concept of a total system approach being presented to Consumer Electronics' management (fig. 104). The study was a major factor in the evolution of the Matchline concept, envisaged as a high-end market range based upon state-of-the-art technology. The name represented three key factors in the systems concept: matching design, the harmonization of all elements; matching controls on all elements whereby all elements would be operated from one remote control; matching in-

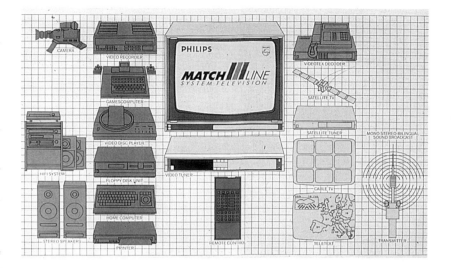

104. Matchline systems concept in a schematic drawing.

105. The Matchline 1 range, from 1983.

106. The Matchline 2 range.

terconnections. The system allowed future technologies, such as satellite broadcasting, to be added later when available.

Thus Matchline 1, which appeared in 1983, introduced the systems approach in television products. It comprised 20 or 26 inch monitors, a separate tuner/source selector, a Video 2000, stereo loudspeakers and a remote control for all units and teletext (fig. 105). Provision was made for connections to other peripherals including a home computer, video disc player, satellite receiver and existing HiFi equipment. In addition a simpler combination of television receivers and VCRs was possible, giving a broad customer choice.

The introduction of Flat Square Tube required new monitors and receivers in Matchline 2 of 1985, the design of which specifically maintained compatibility with the first generation (fig. 106). Infra-red headphones and a switchbox to connect to existing audio equipment were also new features.

Organizational changes within Consumer Electronics reflected the trend towards the integration of audio/video in system form, with a subgroup being formed in the Video Display Products division, under the title of Home Entertain-

ment Systems (HES), which was the commissioner of Matchline 3. The design brief was able to specify the concept in terms going far beyond system TV, to an integrated audio/video system as a result of new technology. This allowed for the reproduction of HiFi stereo on VCR while new laser technology enabled a single component to play back digital audio on Compact Disc and digital audio and video on Compact Disc Video (CDV), and also take the large format video disc. The system also allowed for the trend to more satellite broadcasting systems. CID was given a brief, which fulfilled the original concept of 1981, to design the full range of products: these comprised a range of monitors and receivers, an audio/video receiver, HiFi stereo VCR, CDV remote control system, sound system, satellite receiver, Dolby surround sound processor, as well as 'furniture' to accommodate elements in a space-saving cluster with regard to cable management (fig. 107).

Product management personnel set the specification and design brief and were responsible for bringing the various disciplines together, including development, manufacturing and CID. Article teams or concept teams were formed at the start of the conception phase of the project and the responsible designer from CID, Mike McGourty, was an active member. He points out: 'Not all of the creative work for the designer is done within the confines of his drawing board.'

At formally structured and regular Concept Team meetings, the complex issues such as functional interface between the components were discussed, more detailed specifications of the components made and the first CID sketch proposals were presented (fig. 108). In parallel, regular working discussions took place between the Product Manager, CID designer and the various component 'builders'. With a diverse range of products comprising the system, it was clear that one single design group should have overall responsibility for the design and co-ordination of Matchline, if the intentions behind the product were to be achieved: putting this arrangement in place was complicated but justified by the results. The logistics were complex in all phases of product concept, creation and realization. Product management and CID, both centralized in Eindhoven, had to co-ordinate a range of products developed and manufactured in var-

107. The current Matchline 3 range.

108. A sketch model for Matchline 3: drawings attached to a foam 3D model.

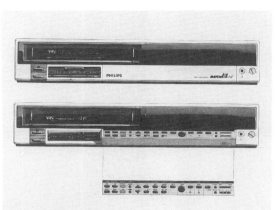

109. Information is easily available as on-screen display and it relates to other graphic elements in the system as well.

110. The remote control unit.

ious centres: Belgium (three centres), Sweden, Germany, Austria, France, Italy, Japan. In the absence of a 'Mechanical System Architect', CID had to assume the role of connector between the various centres, holding regular meetings in Eindhoven with the various component builders, to exchange ideas on construction techniques and choice of materials, with the aim of achieving uniform high quality.

In terms of design philosophy, the concept of an integrated system approach for Audio/Video demanded a new look at the elements. The 'design face' of HiFi has not substantially changed for many years and is basically considered a conventional market in design terms. High-end of the market HiFi is typified visually by hard-edged extruded metal front panels and a multitude of exposed controls and fascia displays. Although generally accepted as connoting quality, this was felt inappropriate for the audio-visual system. In the combination of products in Matchline, one of the major requirements in design terms was to convey a high degree of user-friendliness, emphasizing the convenience of features such as On Screen Display combined with a centralized control interface. The design approach selected was for a softer formal language (so that the forms would in themselves look more user friendly) and to have

111. Information displays on components use clear graphic language, as here on the VCR display.

as few exposed functions on each component (fig. 109). This was intended to emphasize the concept of an interface between the audio and visual aspects of the system and one convenient remote control steering all components from the comfort of an armchair (fig. 110). Where displays were necessary on the components, they matched the quality and readability of On Screen Display by using alpha-numeric displays (fig. 111).

The concept of Matchline is an evolving one and a recent addition to its range is a strikingly innovative, new sound system. Conventional speaker concepts usually consist of two identical boxes, each producing the whole spectrum of the frequency range. The omni-directional sound system devised for Matchline divides the frequency range into a low part and a mid/high part, putting each into different boxes. Because the direction of sound, in terms of stereo reproduction, is not determined for the listener by the low frequencies but by the high ones, frequency units can be put in separate boxes, which offers the advantage of two complete different loudspeaking concepts. A low frequency speaker box together with a pyramid, housing the mid-high frequency units, creates a full-range loud speaker box. A subwoofer concept can be achieved by putting the low frequency speaker boxes together wherever convenient for the user. The two easy-to-place pyramids (fig. 112), the crucial elements determining the stereo image, enables a maximum of sound quality to be achieved in a very small space. The position of the pyramids themselves is less critical than for conventional speaker boxes as they are small and open on all sides, with the sound more directly related to a cone. They can also easily be extended to a 'sound surround' configuration by the addition of two extra satellite pyramids, taking the audio-visual system towards its logical goal of 'home theatre' in terms of the quality and fullness of reproduced sound.

Matchline has been a successful addition to the Philips range: the development of the product shows the complexities of the design management task and the importance of a harmonized policy for achieving successful results (fig. 113).

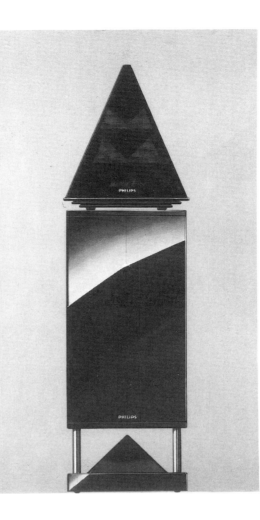

112. The new pyramid speakers and the single low-frequency unit.

113. The current model established as a complete system.

Motorway Tunnel Control and Signalling System

Highways in The Netherlands, as in most countries, have become increasingly overloaded and solutions other than the construction of additional highways needed to be sought. One remedy is informing drivers of problems and speed restrictions, and even of controlling traffic flows.

The purpose of MTCSS is to detect changes in traffic flow patterns and to use this information to help control traffic flows by passing instructions or warnings to drivers through the overhead matrix signs. The information gathered is also used to help plan road maintenance programmes. It is under development at Philips Rugged Systems for the Rijkswaterstaat (RWS),

the Dutch government department responsible for the state's infra-structure of highways and engineering works, like the Deltaworks, rivers, canals, bridges, tunnels, locks, sluices and flood-control dams (fig. 114).

The system was specified by RWS in cooperation with Philips Rugged Systems. Thus, before CID were invited to participate, the choice of hardware components and configuration had been decided upon. Philips Rugged Systems' original request was for CID involvement only with the graphic redesign of the information displayed on the operator screens. The feeling at CID, however, was that with the

114. Example of a current Tunnel Control room before redesign.

functional specification already made, there was not enough freedom in decision taking to justify the investment of time and money. Therefore CID proposed joining the project on the basis of investigating alternative interface components. In addition, instead of designing a dedicated, one-off desk for one control room, CID proposed exploring the possibilities of using the Philips Electronic Office System (PEOS) as the hardware basis for the operator interface. This was accepted as one of the bases for participation.

In order to obtain information about the system and its functions, a small group was established, consisting of two RWS members, a software engineer from the development team of Philips Rugged Systems and a CID designer, Flip Wegner. They met every ten days and, from the point of view of CID, there were two important outcomes. Firstly, the necessary background knowledge about the functions and technical constraints of the system were established, based on what had been already achieved in the project. Secondly, it established a good basis for co-operation and helped introduce the possibility of alternative solutions which went beyond the functional specification, normally a fixed point in the process (fig. 115).

In addition, the designers established contact with the intended users of the system, to obtain reaction on their working conditions. Later, when a model of the interface and some of its functions were available, potential operators were invited for a presentation and discussion on the proposals (fig. 116).

The choice of PEOS for the operator console was based on four criteria. There is an increasing tendency for interface components (such as monitor, keyboard, printer, telephone) to be derived from an office environment, not from an engineering environment as before. PEOS fits this tendency well. Secondly, PEOS gives flexibility and modularity. This is important be-

115. Sketch models for new control room configurations.

116. A prototype installation for user tests.

117. The two monitors, keyboard and mouse selected as interface hardware.

cause operator desks will be placed in different configurations in a number of different control rooms. Thirdly, PEOS enables the creation of a family system, consistent and at an affordable price. Finally, PEOS offers an opportunity for a strong Philips identity to be established for the system.

After trying and testing examples of what could be achieved with alternative interface components, it was decided to change the interface hardware (fig. 117). The five monochromatic low-resolution character oriented 14″ monitors were replaced by two full colour high-resolution bit-mapped 19″ monitors. This choice gave an important graphic freedom. It also reduced the spatial problems to come to a proper configuration of the interface components. Also, the input devices were replaced by one keyboard and mouse, and the rigid presentation on five low-level monitors was replaced by a more flexible window-based presentation of information (fig. 118). The operator will have more means to manipulate information, and therefore the feeling of a system dictating the user will be replaced by the feeling of a user who is in charge.

The approach to the project was therefore based not on hardware design but on the best hardware configuration to satisfy the problems of operator efficiency and comfort. Models to the scale of 1:20 were used to present ideas on the options available on the configurations and their potential advantages. Ideas were presen-

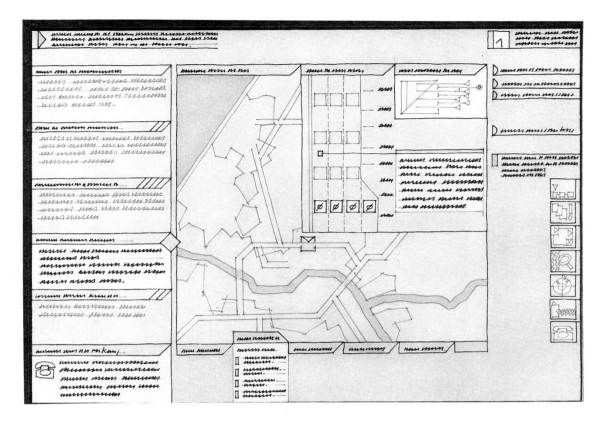

ted to the head of Philips Rugged Systems, who took decisions in consultation with RWS.

The project also represented a considerable change in the relationship of CID with both client and commissioner. What emerged clearly was an identification of the need for earlier involvement in the process of those disciplines involved should at least be Industrial Design, Applied Ergonomics and Graphic Design. There was a growth in awareness that the interface and interaction styles constitute an important part of the total system and can significantly influence the choice of hardware. In other words, a good system from a technical point of view just is not good enough.

The results and changes in the project, its spin-off projects and the changing role of CID prove that industrial design has an important role and responsibility with respect to the user interface aspects of systems and products. The role of CID in projects such as this is changing. Where in the past the role was influencing the aesthetic quality, it is now involved in the earlier stage of the process, helping as part of the design team to define its nature. Thus the auth-

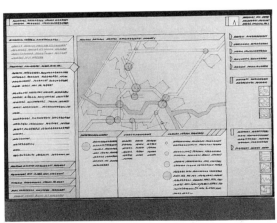

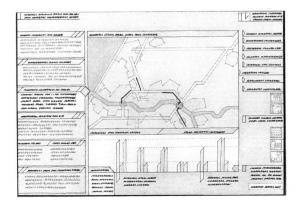

118. Studies of graphic presentation options made during the design phase.

119. The MTCSS system as installed in test lab.

ority of designers is increasing and their influence on functionality aspects becomes greater.

There were also other spin-offs for CID. After the first results became visible, RWS invited CID to design a centralized control system for all vehicle traffic in the western part of the Netherlands, and located on the premises of Benelux tunnel, a main link in the Dutch motorway system. This tunnel will be the first to be equipped with the new MTCSS system. Further projects have led to the RWS commissioning CID to design all control rooms to be rebuilt in the next five to ten years (fig. 119). Thus although a tailor-made system, it has sales potential for other projects.

The MTCSS project can hardly be said to be typical, either of Philips as a whole or the work of CID. However, in the manner in which various aspects of the company's products were brought together and the way design insights and disciplines altered the concept of the project, it has intrinsic interest and could be an indication of a considerable potential for growth in the future.

Philips Electronic Office System

PEOS is a system of support structures specifically designed to harmonize with Philips office equipment. It is an important component of what is known at Philips as 'sophomation', a 'total approach to information management'. In this concept, a user can select that entry point into a comprehensive system which best satisfies his needs, allowing a potential for growth and offering at all stages the best possible solution to information handling and communication problems. Thus the PEOS system not only visually co-ordinates equipment but also solves several important problems, the most obvious of which are cable management and the ergonomic control of comfort in the workplace.

From his many years of experience in the commercial and office furniture and equipment industry, Robert Blaich believed that there was a lack of adequate furniture systems really compatible with automated equipment. It seems to him that an obvious extension of Philips involvement in automated office equipment would

lie in providing the support structures for such equipment. The project did not have an immediate sponsor in one of the Product Divisions, however, and so began as a CID initiative. The first step was to establish a basic research project in CID into office problems, such as providing flexible support components for the variety of Philips electronic equipment and storing the maze of electronic cables necessary for them (fig. 120). The team formed for this end included, in addition to Robert Blaich, Michael McCoy, who heads his own design agency and is co-chairman of the design department of Cranbrook Academy of Art in the USA, Werner Schulze-Bahr, former designer for CID who now has his own design office with several office equipment companies as clients in Kassel, West Germany, and Johnny Lippinkhof, design manager for Telecommunications and Data Systems at CID Eindhoven. One reason for the use of a largely outside team to develop the concept was the existing pressure of projects on CID's

120. An early study scale model for PEOS.

121. A prototype of the cable channel.

own designers: adding the project to the in-house workload would, Robert Blaich estimates, have added eighteen months to the development schedule for that reason alone.

Although from the beginning the support system was seen as part of the Harmonization programme for professional products, at its heart was the need to provide for cable management rather than the emphasis on work surface found in conventional systems (fig. 121). Cable management is achieved by vertical and horizontal channels for cables which are combined within the basic structural system. Connections to a power supply can be made anywhere in a working space, to walls, floors or ceiling. The vertical channels carry cables to equipment

122. Advanced prototype model.

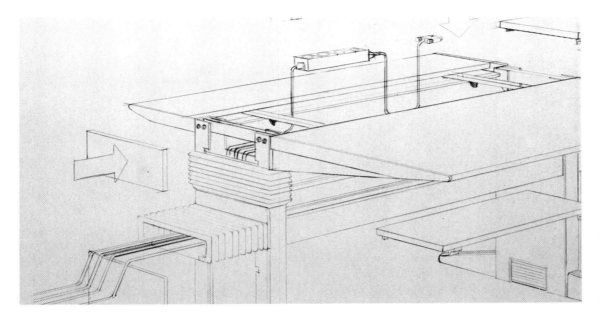

123. Drawings showing the cable organization.

124. Advanced prototype showing placing of equipment.

such as telephones and computers situated at normal working height, while horizontally the components of the system can be linked to form a continuous highly variable network of surfaces, combining complete flexibility with out-of sight storage of cables (fig. 122).

The central elements of the system are the cable beams, two horizontal bridging channels which at the same time also acts as support for the other system elements (fig. 123). The upper channel accommodates cables for equipment required at the work station. These cables are fed into a slot under a rubber lip which ensures that all unnecessary lengths of cable are out of sight in a clean and dry environment. Table-top work stations can be attached to the beam so that electronic equipment can be located wherever it is needed, and backward extensions can be fitted to the beam to give more working depth. These have adaptors for linking ancillary equipment such as lamps, concept housers and monitor arms (fig. 124). Other systems elements, such as conference units, can be fitted to the upper channel; also. The lower cable beam forms a connecting link to other work-stations, carrying power and providing and attachment surface for peripheral equipment such as printers, not needed at the work surface.

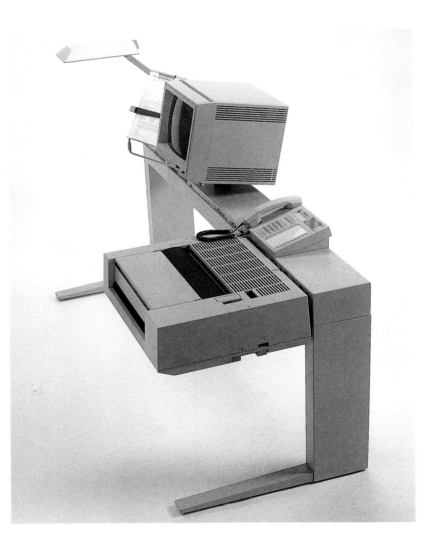

125. Production model showing additional work surfaces attached.

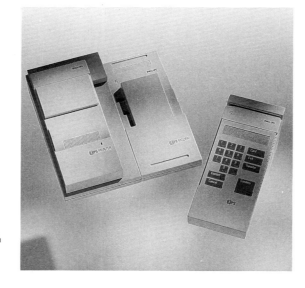

126. Cash register and paying terminal, and credit card cash register, designed to be in line with PEOS in the banking environment.

User comfort also featured prominently in the design process and ergonomic studies were used to specify details of height, angle and distances, as well as the colour of the system. Flexible bellows at connecting points allow for height adjustments to be made either manually in five steps or electronically. Wing nut connections ensure ease of use in securing the elements to the beams, and the modular element of components means that individual and linked work stations can be quickly and easily modified by re-arranging, adding or subtracting components, without the need for specialist fitting or installation. For example, second work surfaces can be attached to a beam to create a double work space (fig. 125). Adjustments to the work station can be easily made by the operator, varying its height to assure a comfortable

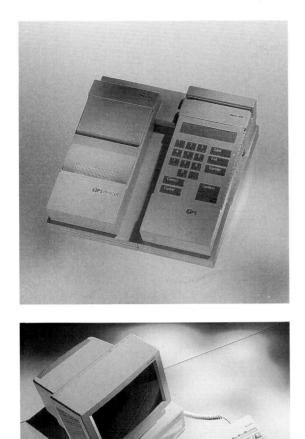

working level. In addition the desk top can be titled down by fifteen degrees from the horizontal plane.

The system was first presented at the Hanover CEBIT Fair in March 1986. In the same year it won the Ergodesign prize at Montreux, Switzerland, awarded by an international jury of ergonomics experts, for its successful integration of ergonomic elements into an innovative and functional system that contributed to 'a better quality of office life'. The Telecommunications and Data Systems Division of Philips became the sponsor of PEOS, and is marketing it through its business supplies network in Europe. The effectiveness of the harmonizing role of the PEOS system is underlined by the fact that it is now used as the standard office system in all TDS product brochures. Although initially designed for office use, PEOS proves its system capability by its application potential in many other contexts. It is well suited for use with Medical Systems products in diagnostic work and in laboratories, for factory work and in special facilities such as control rooms, as with MTCSS (see fig. 115). With the initial design initiative proving so successful, the next stage of the project is under way. Additional storage components, panels, banking work-stations and executive desks, together with a new colour programme are currently being designed, to extend the system for use in a variety of work environments (fig. 127). In addition, a specially designed chair programme will soon be introduced.

127. Executive desk systems.

The Platinum Project

The Platinum project is a code name for a new ultrasound medical equipment system commissioned by Philips Ultrasound Inc. (PUI) of Santa Ana, California. Philips had recently acquired the company, reorganizing the management. The origins of the project were a sense of dissatisfaction with the design tradition that had grown up in the company, against which a market reaction was evident. As to the product, there were problems, for example, with the user interface, in terms of ease of control and the complex array of menus displayed on the monitor screen; new technology had been added but not fully integrated; there were cable management problems; and the lighting and display systems were capable of improvement.

Accordingly the marketing department of PUI drafted an extensive specification, of over 150 typescript pages, for a new ultrasound scanner in 1984 and engaged several consultant designers in competition with each other to generate ideas for the project. The design focus was specified in considerable detail, which can be summarized as creating more relevant information together with a higher quality of information, with shorter operation times and lower operating costs, in a system that could be easily updated, would be easy to use, lightweight and manoeuvreable and have a high-technology image. CID assigned a designer, Antonio Atjak, to ensure the exercise was in conformity with the Philips guidelines for the design of professional equipment. The relationship between Atjak and PUI personnel developed so well that he was supported to visit hospitals in Europe and the USA and the main trade show of medical equipment in Chicago, to familiarize himself with developments in the field (fig. 128).

The outcome of these contacts and visits was a radical design concept devised by Atjak and presented to PUI's director of engineering and the responsible marketing manager in March,

128. Antonio Atjak (standing at the right) with other members of the Platinum development team.

1986 (fig. 129). It was intended as a source of ideas for the consultant designers, but they were unable to implement it. The key problem was that engineers responsible for the electronic system had developed a module so large that its dimensions dominated every consideration, and the industrial designers were unable to cope with it. The problem was recognized and after it had been explained, the engineers accepted a compromise which divided the electronic module into manageable parts, enabling Atjak's radical proposal to be implemented. It was then decided that Antonio Atjak should be placed in charge of the design. The basic considerations influencing his approach were as follows. In the process of ultrasound scanning, the patient is conscious and has to co-operate with the operator's requests, such as to breathe in or out, to hold breath or keep a position. Secondly, two-handed operation is necessary, with the left hand controlling the system and the right hand moving the probe across the patient's body.

Thirdly, images on the monitor screen are not readily easy to interpret. An excellent knowledge of anatomy is required and interpretation

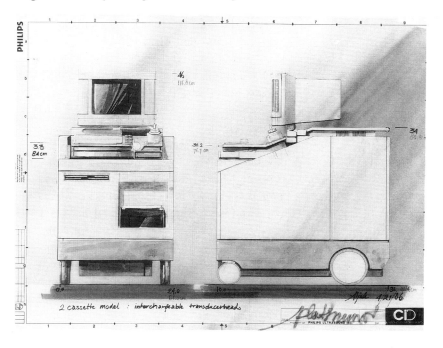

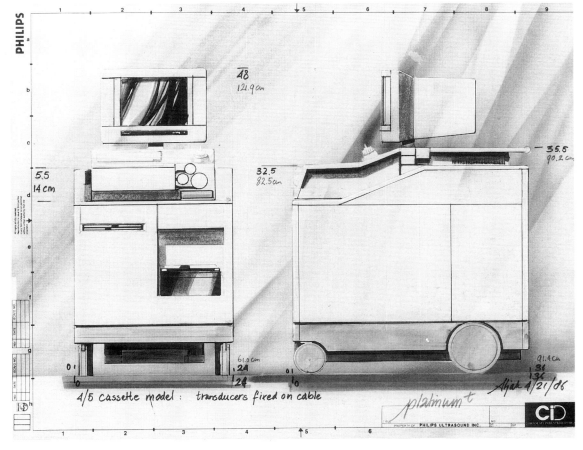

129. Studies prepared by Atjak to develop the final briefing for Platinum.

is a complex process. Fourthly, images can be enhanced, but to do so the operator has to understand the technical parameters of the process. Fifthly, while the machine is capable of documenting and recording information, the operator has to know how to interpret and apply such material. Finally the diagnostic interpretation is made by a doctor, who is in many cases not the operator of the system. The operator has to anticipate each doctor's requirements which can vary a lot.

The conditions under which the apparatus would be used were also analyzed in detail. These included considerations about the operator's position and the tools and procedures used in a wide diversity of applications; the circumstances of patients and environments, both of which could be highly varied. The spatial requirements of operating the apparatus were a critical consideration, particularly since the possibility of building in a range of peripheral equipment had to be considered. Mobility was another obvious requirement, with a need to steer the equipment in a confined space, and have adequate braking for inclined surfaces and when stationary.

130. Model for Platinum.

In essence, Atjak's proposal was for a control panel and display, with the probes and gel required for scanning mounted on a two-link counter-balanced arm, the whole set on a cart. The arm on which the probes were to be mounted was very similar to those found on dental apparatus, and a company was found which undertook to develop this item (fig. 130).

A fundamental consideration was the so-called triangle of interest, the interaction between operator, patient and controls (fig. 133). The controls must be effective but not so dominant they prevent the operator from interacting with the patient. This meant that apparatus had to be brought closer to the patient and the control and display system considerably simplified. A feature of the Platinum proposal was that the control console and monitor could be raised and lowered, or move out and shifted laterally in order to provide an optimum working position under any circumstances (see figs. 64, 131 for the studies used for this). This flexibility of control positions gives the operator the ability to choose what configuration is appropriate for the patient under a large range of situations. Some equipment of this type has two monitor screens, which require a greater degree of attention from operators, diverting them from the patient.

Platinum has only one monitor and very simple controls, but at the same time it enables all presently known ultrasound techniques to be applied and also all those at present envisaged. Two important developments were crucial to the practicality of the concept. The designer invented a means of retracting the cables connecting the probe to the system into a small package, this later evolved into an exchangeable cable cassette. Later, engineering also made a major contribution, with a detachable probe system which enabled a large array of different probes to be available on the control panel and connected at will.

To demonstrate the feasibility of the concept, an accurate cardboard mock-up was built (fig. 132). It showed the structure in detail, the position of components, and even the way the cosmetic panels could be mounted. It allowed applications specialists in marketing to scrutinize

131. Studies for the control monitor.

its handling in actual conditions of use, an exercise which was documented in photographs. As the concept became more clearly defined, it was obvious there would be considerable costs involved. Consequently, the photo-documentation was sent to a number of doctors known to be very sceptical about new developments. This was a rigorous test, but from it enough confidence was gained to pursue the concept. Coincidentally, an article appeared in a medical journal on the ergonomic factors involved in ultrasound scanners that advised manufacturers to do almost exactly what was being developed at PUI. This further underlined the project's viability.

With the concept secured, time was spent improving the detailing, particularly of the user interface. Several people were involved but Judy Gatinella was largely responsible for establishing the philosophy and hierarchy of the control system (fig. 133). Studies were undertaken, for example, to establish which controls were necessarily used with a high, medium or low frequency of use. Therefore the sequence of user operations was related to the disposition of the controls. The overall intention was to allow more freedom of control to operators and at the same time greater ease of use. A consultant was contracted to help generate the drawings and build the final model. This was presented to a review meeting with some thirty participants from different departments and caused a great deal of excitement.

Considerable time was spent designing the screen graphics for the control and display part of the user/interface, which was developed by

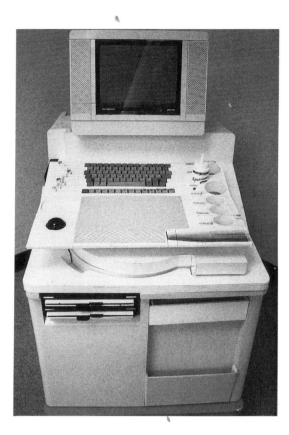

132. The cardboard mock-up used to test handling under actual conditions.

the applications specialist/product manager and software engineers. Proposals for this aspect were equally as radical as the physical structure, concentrating a wide array of functions onto a single screen, but allowing easy recognition and simple control (fig. 134).

In September, 1986, prototype parts began to come in and several adjustments were made, although the finished product remains very similar to the final model. Throughout the process, excellent support was given by the engineering department. Review meetings were held every two to three months and when Antonio Atjak was not in California, close contact was maintained by telephone and telefax as details and accessories were designed.

In all presentations, whether for internal review or for potential customers, the user interface, in which industrial design has played an important role, has earned considerable attention and respect. The functional versatility of the Platinum and its distinctive image have broken all PUI sales records for a system prior to

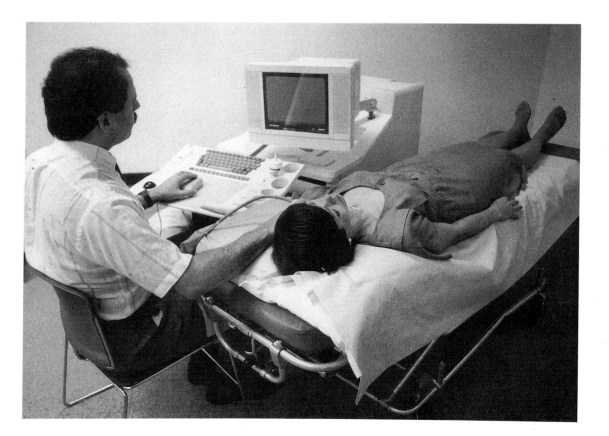

133. Studies for the interaction between patient, operator and controls.

market launch (fig. 135). A feature of the Platinum project as a whole has been a remarkably high degree of interchange and co-operation between the design function represented by Atjak and all aspects of PUI's structure and operations. The role of Dennis Paul, Product Manager for the Platinum project and former operator of ultrasound equipment, was of particular importance in the development of the solution. Platinum was introduced in late 1988 and its success illustrates the value and necessity of capable project management in ensuring that designers, alongside other specialists, fully contribute to the product development process.

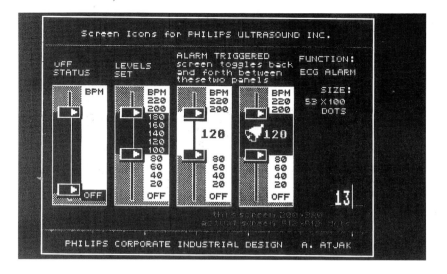

134. Studies for the screen graphics.

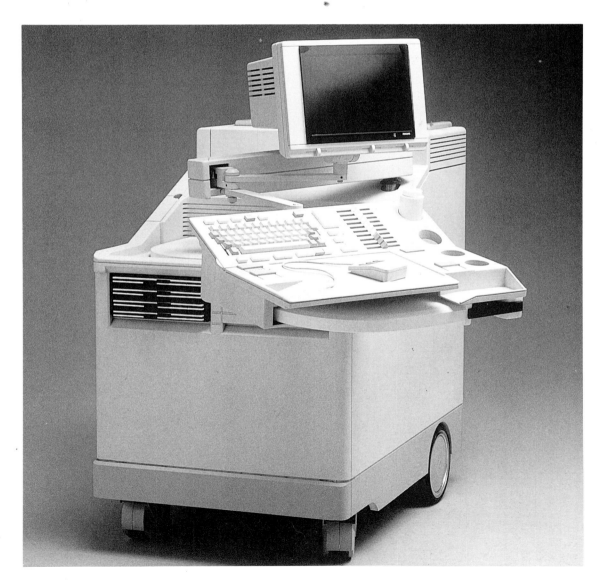

135. The final Platinum prototype.

Professional Video Cameras

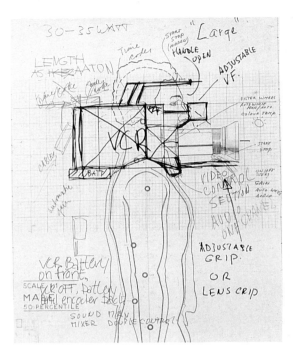

136. A design concept sketch made during the workshop.

In early February 1985, the product group IPG Cameras of Philips I & E, Breda, held a workshop for portable camera design. This was a preliminary step in the design of new video cameras. The initiative for this came from the availability of new technology, and the problem was how to apply the technology most effectively in the design of video cameras. The workshop was intended to gain as much material as possible about the work of cameramen in news gathering and location work, by drawing on their experience with portable cameras and their perceptions of what was required in terms of camera handling. This would give the design, development and marketing departments at Philips a much clearer understanding of what the market required.

Professional cameramen, development engineers, a human factors specialist and representatives of CID and commercial departments

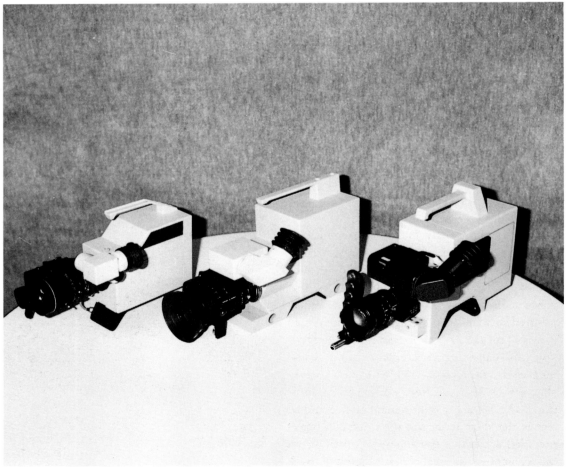

137. The foam dummy models made overnight for evaluation by the workshop.

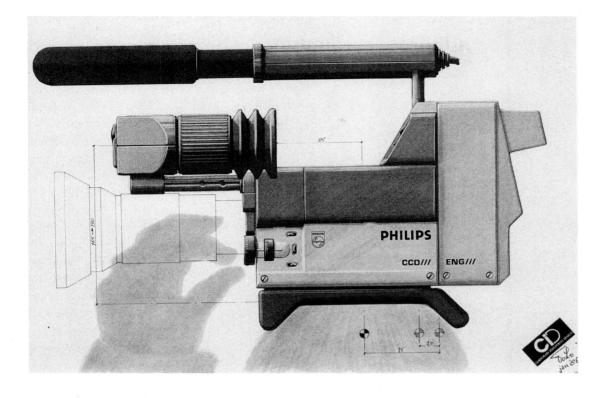

138. Concept sketch made on basis of workshop trials.

139. Foam dummy based on the concept sketches.

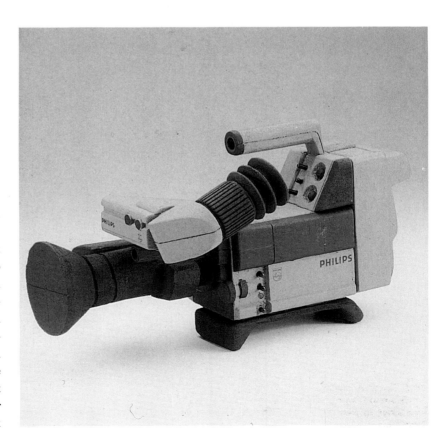

were therefore brought under the leadership of a training department representative for five days. After preliminary discussions and brainstorming sessions on the needs of cameramen, the participants were divided into three groups, each under a designer from CID, to design a camera incorporating their ideas (fig. 136). Models were rapidly made overnight to be used on the next day for further comparison and development (fig. 137). In considering the design criteria, two obviously important factors were weight and balance. Other ideas incorporated were a low front line to the camera, and the position of the viewfinder in relation to it, so that views to the right were not blocked. The need to position switches to guard against unintentional use, and for the grip to be secure and comfortable, also came up for consideration. These and numerous other points emerged from the workshop discussions and were worked on in detail (fig. 138). Not every requirement cited could be met in the short term, but the workshop report provided a bank of invaluable information for the designers, so that further detailed work

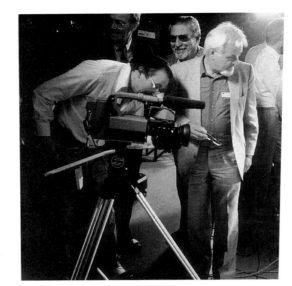

could proceed in full confidence that the basic direction was soundly established (fig. 139). Another factor highlighted by the workshop was the need for close co-operation between the designer and the development engineer, since the inside of the camera would be packed with electronic equipment with no free space, and the overall dimensions and disposition of components was critical.

In June 1986 the workshop members were invited back again for three days to examine three experimental working cameras that had been constructed in the interim (fig. 140). The party was again divided into three groups, but on this occasion each went out with a journalist on location to follow up actual news stories. After this

140. The handbuilt prototypes being evaluated during the second workshop.

141. The final product, the LDK 90.

work experience the results were discussed and evaluated, and modifications suggested. The immediate general reaction was however very positive.

For the actual production of the cameras, Philips had entered into a joint business venture with Bosch under the name of Broadcast and Television Systems (BTS) and the first fruits of the workshop appeared in 1987 under that name as the LDK 90 system (fig. 141). LDK 90 had a high quality technical specification, and was compact and light, weighing under two and a half kilograms (under five pounds)which with lens and batteries increased to six and a half kilograms (under fifteen pounds). Essential controls were designed to be ready to hand, while others were placed behind a safe flap. The ergonomically shaped handle could also be used as a microphone holder. The camera was adaptable to a wide variety of working situations and had a good range of technical options.

One of the participants in the workshop, Hans Brouwer of NOB (Nederlands Omroep-produktie Bedrijf) contributed a review of the camera to *Zerb,* the journal of the Guild of Television Cameramen. He wrote that 'the low height of the camera and the specially shaped viewfinder allow an unlimited view to the right, a luxury for the cameraman. Due to the flat camera base, the cameraman has the option of using the camera with or without shoulderpad. Without the use of the shoulderpad, the camera is easily balanced out on the shoulder when lenses of different weights are used. As far as I know the LDK 90 is the only camera which feels comfortable on the shoulder with and without recorder.' It was, he concluded, a 'cameraman's camera'. This judgment would seem to be supported by sales figures which at the time of writing exceeded four-fold the original projections.

The entire development process had taken less than two years, in itself noteworthy for a complex piece of equipment. Equally importantly, the experience gained could be adapted to the design of other professional cameras. More directly, the workshop approach and the information derived from the LDK 90 were to be invaluable in the development of a production camera designated the LDK 900. Rough foam

models were made before cameramen from five countries were invited to a preliminary workshop which drew on their perceptions and experiences. The ergonomics of the apparatus emerged as a prime consideration in ensuring ease of operation and freedom of use to obtain the most difficult shots. The technology available made it possible to conceive of a studio camera with reduced dimensions, moving towards the standards achieved in video cameras. The reduction in development time is also noteworthy: the LDK 900 project began in May, 1987, and the product was launched at a major trade fair in April 1988.

During the development of the LDK 900, the industrial designer assigned to the project, Floor Levendig, used it in his CAD training programme, and after the workshop was held presented all design ideas through the medium of CAD photos, slides and hard copy (fig. 142). The main advantage he found was that it was possible to make a clear and realistic presentation of what a product would look like, and to show possible modifications. The technical development of the camera went in parallel with the design, and Levendig again worked closely with the engineers, to produce visualizations for presentation to commercial staff, thus ensuring

142. A CAD design for the LDK 900 studio camera.

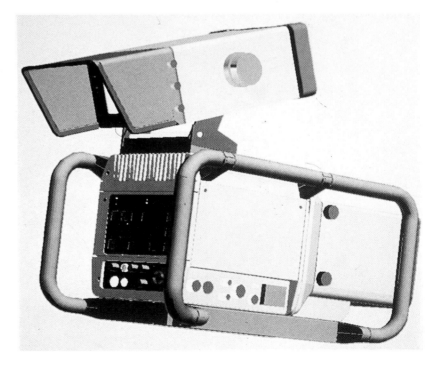

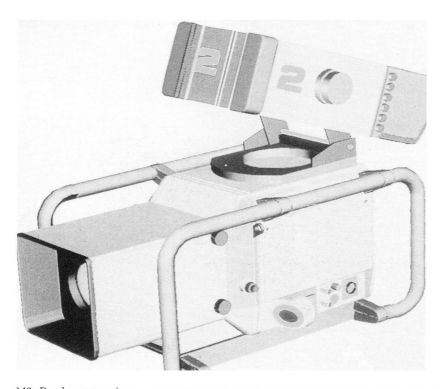

143. Developments using CAD.

the possibility of fast decision-making (fig. 143).

With a high performance technical specification, the extra attention given to the needs of the final users of the camera resulted in an effective and very competitive apparatus. The time and cost spent in the early stages meant that expensive mistakes were avoided, and there were benefits in terms of development time (fig. 144). Indeed the project illustrates very clearly the advantages of 'getting it right first time'. If the input of effort and energy in the preliminary stages provides a more effective basis of information, the application of CAD techniques also demonstrates the possibilities of rapidly capitalizing on those advantages, and giving a capacity for quick response throughout the development process. In both respects the video camera project demonstrates important principles which are applicable to and adaptable to other areas of design.

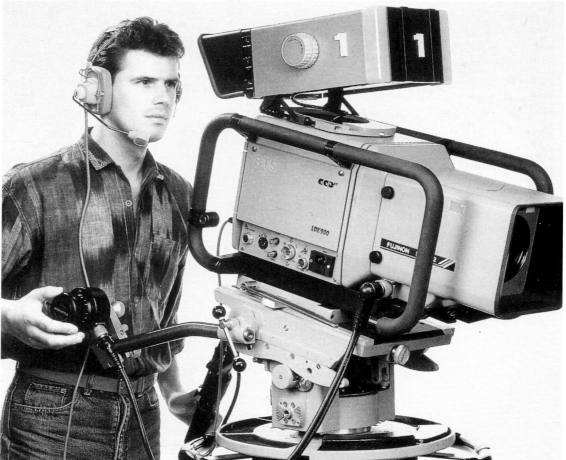

144. The final production model LDK 900.

Roller Radio and Moving Sound

The Roller Radio represents a fundamental change of mentality within Philips, for its lighthearted fun design, directed at a youth market is without precedent. Within CID it has been likened to a breath of fresh air. It began as a student project by Graham Hinde, who in 1982 was studying product design at Kingston Polytechnic, London. For a second year project the students were asked to design a radio recorder with detachable cassette player capable of use as a portable product of the Walkman type, at as low a price as possible. After graduating, Graham Hinde joined Philips design offices at Croydon in England, where his original design for the Roller Radio was noticed by Robert Blaich and Peter Nagelkerke, Design Manager of Consumer Electronics (fig. 145).

They saw it as a product with specific youth

145. Graham Hinde's original concept for the Roller radio.

146. Early foam model for the Roller, exploring relationship between handle, speakers and cassette unit.

connotations, a simple, colourful fun project, which coincided with a process under way at Philips to rejuvenate their brand image with young consumers. Market research had shown that Philips did not have a good image with young people, being considered by them too serious and traditional. A youth Task force had been established by the company to tackle this problem, and the Roller concept was presented to them. Robert Blaich, by then Chairman of the Youth Task Force, and Leo van Leeuwen, General Manager of Personal Audio, were enthusiastic and gave the project strong support.

Initially a number of sketches and models were made as alternative solutions to the basic concept of a fixed handle and prominent, round loudspeakers, though the original form proved to have the strongest impact (fig. 146). Subsequently Murray Camens, then Senior Product Designer for Personal Audio began with

Graham Hinde, whose main responsibilities were still in television design, to refine the form and incorporate the existing Philips tape deck mechanism. The detachable cassette player in the original concept was not included, as this would have made the product too expensive, taking it out of the targeted market group. Camens added strong detailing to the speaker covers, and at the same time associated them with roller-skate wheels, to give the product an even more youthful and playful character. The final model drawing was made by Camens, with two colours, red and yellow, proposed, the handle and speaker details being the colourway (fig. 147). The graphics and the Roller logo were designed by Bob Vranken, Product Graphic Design, CID. They were simple but lively, and thus in complete harmony with the product. The finished radio is predominantly injection moulded, with foil-printed speaker

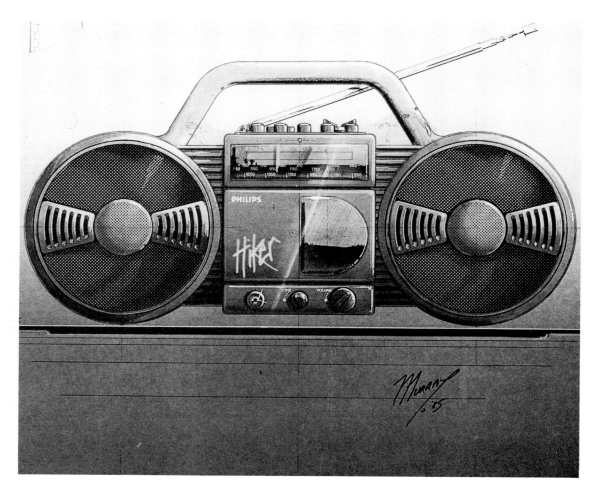

147. Final sketch drawing of colour proposal for Roller I.

148. Back view of production model Roller showing 'roller-skate' effect on speakers.

149. The black Roller, proposed for a slightly older market.

rings and silkscreen product graphics (fig. 148).

The Roller radio was an initiative of the Youth Task Force, for whom it, like the Tracer Two shaver, was a key youth product. Initially the sales forecasts were cautious, but this perception of the product changed when five times the target figures were ordered even before production began. The success of the Roller has changed Philips' image in a significant and positive way in the youth market, and it has encouraged CID designers to believe that Product Managers will be more adventurous in accepting new design ideas in the future. Putting 'fun' into Philips products was not a concept that was easily accepted. According to Peter Nagelkerke, however, the Roller has also had a far-

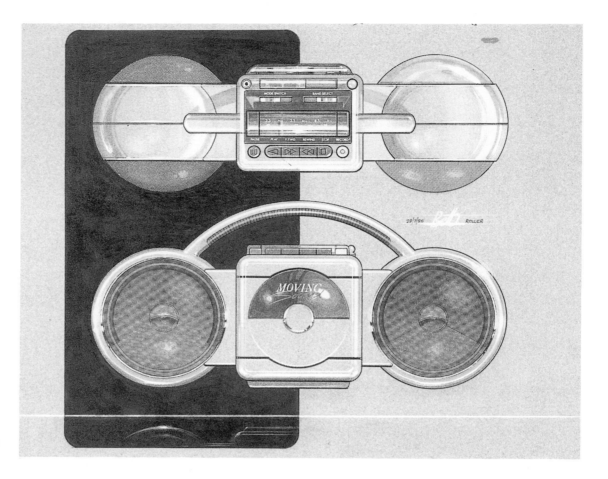

150. A drawing and a foam
model for Roller Two.

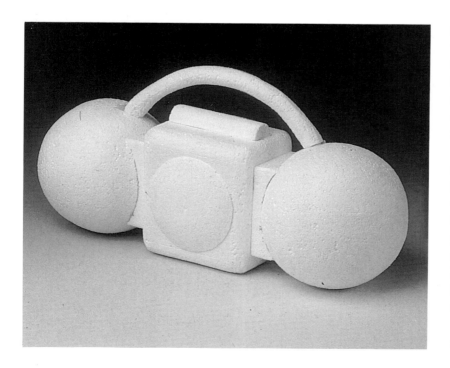

reaching impact on the design mentality within
CID. He believes that there is little value in
competing with the Japanese on the basis of
their typical approach of *Kai Zen,* the step-by-
step improvement of a product. Instead he
advocates a more radical approach to product
innovation.

The success of the Roller has led to a number
of alternative colour and graphic executions, as
market research showed that the youth market
could be further subdivided. For example, there
is a baby pink model intended to appeal to
young girls, and a more sophisticated all black
model for the somewhat older consumer (fig.
149). A second generation of the Roller has also
been marketed, including a double cassette
deck version (fig. 150).

Out of the success of the Roller camera range
of products under the title of Moving Sound.

151. The Moving Sound range of products.

152. Part of the second Moving Sound range with white as basic colour.

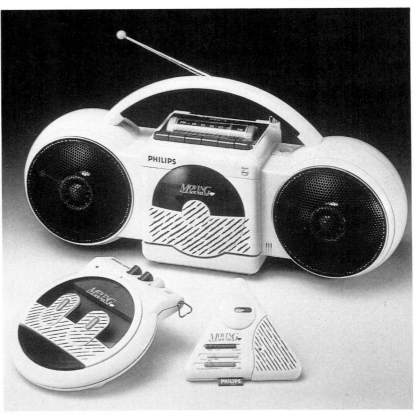

This was a full scale strategy programme initiated by the Personal Audio Group under the direction of Leo van Leeuwen, aimed at strengthening brand preference for Philips among young consumers. The underlying concept is that consumers make their first choices at a young age and begin then to establish long term brand preferences and loyalties. In collaboration with CID, the Personal Audio group developed a brief for a number of products, to be brought together under a common image, reasoning that young people see many products in the same way as clothing, and that therefore the products in the range should be innovatively stylish, fashionable and desirable, so fitting the accepted patterns of expectation. The role of CID was to provide a totally co-ordinated approach to product design and marketing, an approach, according to Robert Riphagen, new to Philips (fig. 151).

Murray Camens and Cameron Robinson designed a graphic presentation for the new Moving Sound range, with the colour yellow chosen for products onto which the 'torn paper' graphics

153. Packaging and point of sale details for Moving Sound Two.

154. The Moving Sound style guide.

conceived by Robinson were applied.

The packaging for the range, by Terry Ducay and Harry Arens, CID Packaging Group, was intended to provide strong support for product presentation at the point of sale. Market research shows that the Moving Sound campaign has been instrumental in greatly improving Philips' image with the targeted audience of young people, while sales have been higher than anticipated. The second range of Moving Sound audio products, launched in early 1988, was a logical continuation of the first series (fig. 152). Graphic work on the second range of eight products began with a workshop in which a number of young Philips graphic designers participated. The brief from product management specified an eye catching, fashionable appearance. The target market was boys and girls in the ten to fifteen years age bracket (the first range had appealed more to girls than to boys). The existing logo was continued but there was a clear need for a new visual link to be developed between the different products and packaging. Gary Grimes was appointed Contact Designer for Personal Audio; for product graphics, Marcel Heijen and Ton Batussen worked with him. Alan Palmer was Contact Designer for packaging, with Marja Zuurman.

In the chosen design, a dark grey pattern of stripes has been partly applied to all the products, which are predominantly white with black accent areas such as speaker grilles, cassette doors and so on. A cat silhouette has been added to the moving Sound logo and two accent colours, pink and green, applied to knobs and buttons. This image was continued and accentuated in the packaging, which included shelf displays for the larger products. The stripes became a background pattern in black and white, the cat was repeated as a fun element and a zigzag teeth element was introduced to divide white and black and give a hint of aggressiveness (fig. 153).

As soon as the design had been agreed upon, CID took the initiative of designing a Style Guide, a loose-leaf binder containing a description, examples and artwork for reproduction of all the graphic elements so that each Philips organization and advertising agency had the basic visual materials when developing publicity and advertising material (fig. 154).

In any policy of segmenting markets it is necessary to adapt the design approach to each group of users. What is perhaps one of the most noteworthy features of this project is that the distinctive visual qualities of the Roller Radio and of Moving Sound have been carefully and creatively designed for young people by young designers in CID. They were deliberately chosen by age and given the freedom to express themselves in ways relevant to their consciousness of themselves and their generation. Behind what has been a considerable success is a close and continuous co-operation between design and marketing, and above all a management perception of design potential that was given its opportunity.

Arena Vision

Television and film recording of major sports events regularly include close-ups and slow-motion shots, making viewers more aware of the outstanding skills involved. Professional sportsmen and women have thereby become actors, with sport more like a theatrical performance and in both the audience is an indispensable point of reference.

In the modern sports stadium, the distances between spectators and players can often be great. Lighting can help to concentrate the attention of spectators and dramatize the event and for television broadcasting lighting can create a range of effects. This needs a flexible lighting system, in which care must be taken to avoid disturbing players and spectators with glare that can hamper performance or cause discomfort. Environmental considerations are also important, with a need to avoid light spillage troubling people and traffic inn the vicinity of a stadium.

To satisfy all these demands Philips decided to develop one new sports light to replace the earlier model, developed in 1987 (fig. 155). The new light would be a compact single housing luminaire capable of adaptation to different optical combinations of high technical specification. The light was developed by a product team comprising various disciplines, including the Commercial Department (Outdoor Lighting), Lamp Development, Applications Department, Light Technical Department, Technical Development and CID, represented by Henk Schellens, Design Manager for the Lighting Division, and the designer Gerrit Arts. This team met regularly after the inception of the project in January 1987.

The optical system on which the concept was based was highly advanced and the brief required the design to embody this quality: the keywords involved were advanced, instrumental, high-tech, modern and professional. These qualities had to be made evident through the form, materials and colours chosen, in the intention that with advanced technology and design, the luminaire being created should last into the twenty-first century. Specific require-

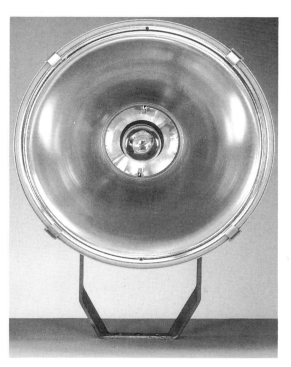

155. The earlier model stadium light.

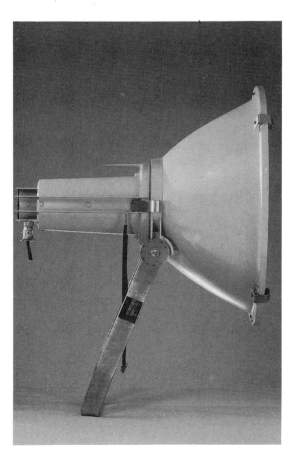

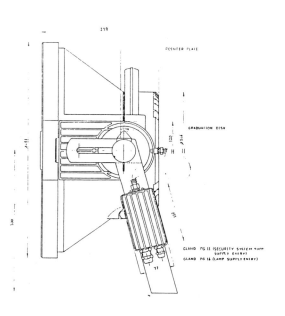

ments were that the light should be capable of being mounted on masts or banisters, hanging as well as standing, that it be lightweight and portable, have easy mounting and maintenance, and be easily adjusted when mounted. The light technical requirements specified 1800 watt metal halide lamps and four different reflectors for mounting heights from twenty to fifty metres above ground. A new halide lamp formed the basis for development from which the overall technical concept was established by the product team. This concept served as the starting point for the designers to begin defining the first form studies.

A variety of formal studies were presented by means of sketches and foam models, enabling the product team to make preliminary decisions before a first model was made (fig. 156). This was shown to an international working group of different European marketing managers. Observations ane requests from this group were embodied in a new model, executed in more detail and from actual materials. In addition to drawings, sketches and foam models, CID used computer aided design as a tool (fig. 157). At

156. Arena vision technical sketch.

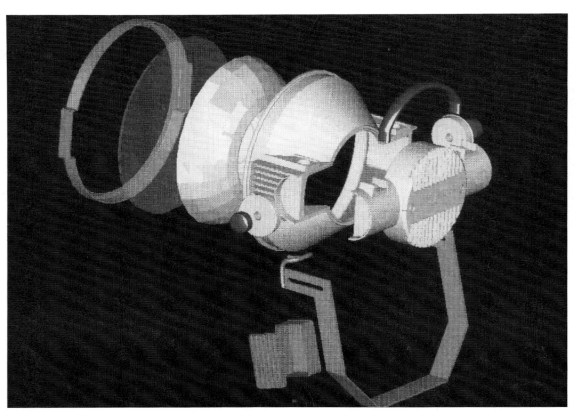

157. CAD designs for Arena Vision.

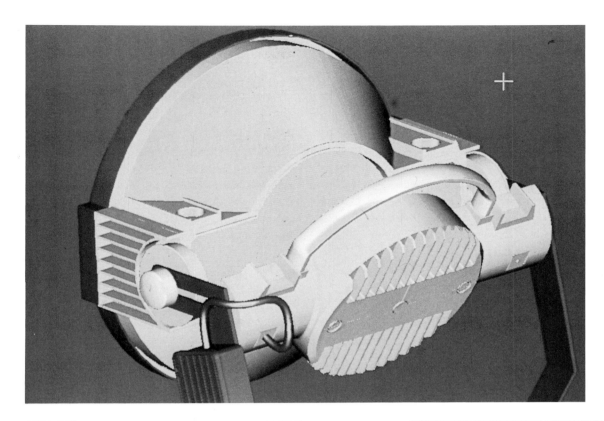

the same time the technical department prod-uced a working model for the purpose of test measurements on temperature (fig. 158), wind sensitivity, mechanical aspects, suitability pro-duction, ease of change of lamps, and so forth. The final model which emerged from this det-ailed process of design and testing embodied advanced lighting, optical and manufacturing

technologies with a complex, high-performance specification.

The approved design (fig. 159) consists of two main parts, both made from high-pressure die-cast aluminium with a natural blasted finish: the front reflector housing has a mounting bracket to which a separate connection box is attached, and the read reflector housing is per-

158. Computer generated images showing details and temperature patterns in the light fixture.

manently attached to the front by a hinge and two stainless steels clips, which can be opened when necessary for relamping or servicing (fig. 160). The front glass, chemically toughened, is protected by a stainless steel wire mesh (fig. 161) which in case of breakage prevents large pieces of glass from falling out. The black lacquered bracket can be mounted either upright or hanging, and is adjustable in any direction. The rear housing has a blue lacquered grip, enabling it to be easily carried by hand. After loosening securing clips it can be also used to position the housing. Safe relamping and servicing is achieved by a snap-in electrical connector, which automatically disconnects the power when the floodlight is opened.

This metal halide variable floodlight is called the MVF 406, and production models were introduced in **August 1988, at the Philips** Stadium in Einhoven, the home of the Philips S.V. football team.

Negotiations are underway for the use of the light in several sports stadia, for lighting the 1992 Olympic Games at Barcelona, and for other applications.

Sports lamps are frequently positioned on high pylons, and are indistinct as a form to anyone below (fig. 162). 'Out of sight, out of mind', runs an old adage, and consequently such products have been conceived in the past in purely technical terms. The addition of an industrial designer to the product team was not primarily to improve the visual appearance of the product, though this should not be underestimated in communicating the values of the product to potential purchasers. More importantly, the designer's role has been to contribute to improving the efficacy of the fitting in terms of installation, servicing and performance. Many fitters working in exposed situations in all kinds of weather conditions, may feel the resulting benefit.

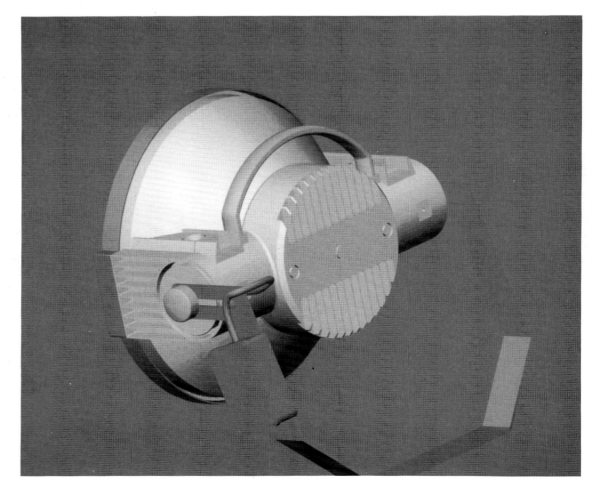

159. Final design studies.

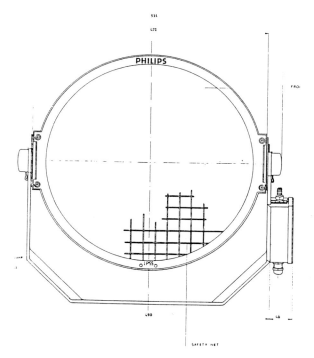

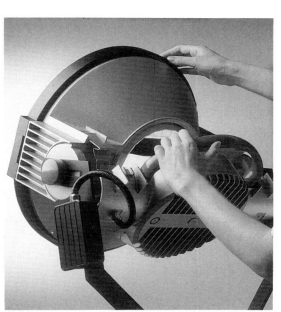

161. Drawing for the protective mesh.

160. The final product, showing housing of units.

162. The new lamp and the earlier model. Note the smaller size, particularly valuable as regards windage, and consequent lower need for supporting mast strength.

Vacuum Cleaners

In 1982, work began on a new range of Philips sledge vacuum cleaners under the direction of Lou Beeren, Design Manager, DAP. The aims of the project were threefold, to apply new developments in electronics, materials and systems, to create an attractive design with the possibility of maximum model and type differentiation and to remove existing deficiencies in particular by providing an improvement in the dust bag volume and filtering, allowing for accessory storage to be incorporated, and for reducing noise levels, weight and volume while allowing for greater power where required in the model range (fig. 163, 164).

Philips had entered the European vacuum cleaner market in the 1950s through the acquisition of two Dutch companies, Ruton and Erres. Their early models were cylinder cleaners on slides which evolved in the 1960s into boxier shapes with the swivel top connection for the hose, considered a revolutionary innovation on its introduction in 1964. Later, new developments in styrene and acrylic plastic compounds, and parallel advances in complex moulding technology led to the transition from metal construction to the thermoplastic components used today.

In the early stages of redesigning the product

163. Previous model of vacuum cleaner.

164. Sketches for the case model.

165. Pre-development foam model.

range a broad approach to a range of options was adopted, which was narrowed down as the concepts became more clearly defined. Extensive discussions were held within CID and with the technical and commercial disciplines involved, drawing on their extensive experience, and using research and tests. The organizations cooperating on the project included Philips Research Laboratories, the main reserch organization, as well as the development group and the application laboratory at Hoogeveen, where vaccum cleaners are manufactured and which carried out the field tests. Consumer research, to establish the range structure, market research, for trends and signals regarding what was acceptable in the market, the service department and the general advertising department also contributed to the development.

An important question was that of noise reduction. Initial studies were carried out by

166. Plastic dummy model.

168. The T500 model vacuum cleaner.

Philips Research Laboratories. Their conclusion was that attaching a reactive muffler would significantly reduce noise radiation — that is noise escaping from the compressor of the cleaner through the air outlets — to a low level in terms of both volume and frequency. A muffler was developed which as well as being efficient and practical, gave complete freedom to the industrial designers. Further reduction in noise was also made possible by insulation and by setting the motor on large flexible rubber mountings.

Other components of the cleaner were subjected to detailed analysis with a view to establishing the range of possibilities open as a basis for further decision making. These components included the motor, the type of dust bag, the cord storage unit, hose pipes and tubes and suction accessories, as well as operational elements such as switches and regulators. With each component decisions had to be taken on whether existing components were still satisfactory, whether they needed to be developed further or whether completely new components had to be created. The formal arrangement of the different elements also required detailed consideration, for example whether the dust storage system should be front loading or top loading, where the motor and the cord storage should be positioned, and where accessories should be stored. Each such aspect also had to be considered in terms of the total range structure. Various possibilities for the overall formal concept were also considered and three were explored in some detail. These were the sledge, the sledge and stick and the case model. The final decision was to develop the case model further (figs. 164-166).

The range, it was decided, would comprise three basic models. The lower range, designated the T300, would be developed later, though linked to the rest of the range. The medium range and upper range models, designated T500 and T700 respectively, would have the following features: a new, top-loading dust storage system, a new swivel top, storage space for accessories and a range of control features. A derivation of the T500 was also created for special outlets under the designation T400: its lower housing and internal components would remain in common (figs. 167-169).

169. The T700 model vacuum cleaner.

167. The T400 model vacuum cleaner.

The T700 model was intended for production in three or four variants, with a new standard motor giving improved air displacement and vacuum, and a very low noise level. The model obviously needed to be differentiated visually from the T500 range, so as to create an impression of quality. A distinct accessory compartment at the rear of the apparatus, together with provision for increased dust capacity resulted in a product of increased length and therefore larger wheels were used to maintain the proportions within the overall dimensions (fig. 170). User function, such as the large foot control and the electronic displays were given special attention, the computer control displays being integrated behind a transparent acrylic strip, with the electronic indicator lamps clearly visible during use, but almost imperceptible when switched off. The total dimensions of the pro-

170. Detail of wheels and storage unit on the T700.

duct remained within acceptable limits, its colour and product graphic treatment remained subdued but sophisticated, clearly reflecting not only the quality of the product but also emphasizing its additional features. Two models in the T500 range also provided a compact and modern cleaner with a competitive range of features and accessories, so completing the first stage of the range (fig. 171).

The extent of co-operation on this project has been one of its notable features. In addition, the ground work undertaken and decisions made have considerable implications for further developments, since the work so far has established the essential parameters with which the range of products is being further extended. This aspect typifies the management of many projects at Philips at the present time. The pattern is for intensive development to which considerable resources are committed in the crucial development stage. This allows in turn for a later process of diversification and response to be based securely on the potential of the initial work undertaken.

171. The current product range.

PART 4

CONCLUSION

The projects discussed in the previous section were selected to show the spectrum of design management questions which have to be faced at Philips. Many others would be needed to convey the full range. What is clear, however, is that the practice of design management in any company cannot be understood outside the context of that company's history, its overall management structure and policy, its market position, and its product range. Some particular aspects of the Philip's experience will therefore not be transferable to other organizations. Nevertherless, certain principles can be identified which have general relevance. Above all, it is obvious that design cannot make an effective contribution in any company unless there is strong understanding and support for it at the highest levels of management. The support which over the years has underpinned all the developments in Philips design and which

172-4 These three products (workstation, information entry pad and terminal) are part of research into the office of the future.

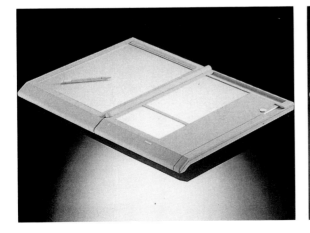

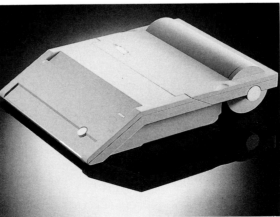

strongly continues today has been of inestimable value.

Of equal importance is the need to integrate the design function into the activities of a company at all levels. Its initial introduction at Philips saw design used as a late, superficial addition in the product development process, with insufficent contact and cooperation with engineering and marketing. In that respect it was typical of its time. Times change, however, and yesterday's accepted practice became today's problem. Although overnight solutions are rarely feasible, change can be brought about by effective management. Recognizing the problem, establishing a structure and responsibilities to provide a remedy, and constantly working at all levels for greater co-operation, is yielding significant benefits for CID and indeed throughout Philips. A key concept in this re-

175-6. Two views of the Philips Home interactive System, which provides a range of connexions with information and entertainment systems (television, radio, video, cable, satellite, telefax, CD & videodisc, among others) with a computer system.

spect is that of design manager, responsible for liaison and communication between design and other disciplines, which has proved to be an excellent means of dealing with the problem of linkages across departmental and disciplinary boundaries.

Another important factor is the need for designers to be aware of the market for which they are working, and capable of closely defining the actual and latent needs of potential customers. The Tracer project shows in this respect the importance of pooling information at an early stage and the value of an overview which enables a project devised for one market to be adapted to another. The coffee makers study, on the other hand, shows how careful identification of market segments and redesign to meet their needs is used to maintain share in a saturated market. The development of professional video cameras, with a small, clearly identifiable market, saw designers, together with users, able to define jointly the nature of what the product ought to be. Philips solution of identifying global market segments (as with the Youth Task Force) rather than national groups has certainly signigicantly benefitted from the input and insights provided by designers.

It is also clear that designers need to be aware of the technology at their disposal and able to positively harness it for an improved solution to a problem. The MTCSS project revealed designers not only improving the ergonomics of a control room, but stimulating an improved specification for both hardware and software. In the case of Arena Vision and the LDK 900, the designers not only used CAD to shape the product, but to help identify a range of options and reduce development times.

The above factors all relate to the operation of the design funtion within the company. Philips also offers some pointers to the ways design can contribute to the company as a whole. In this respect, harmonization is of twofold importance. For example, a hospital which buys Philips medical equipment is likely to buy Philips office equipment for its administration if there is a perceivable continuity between the two ranges. A perception of quality in one product area has tangible benefits in other product

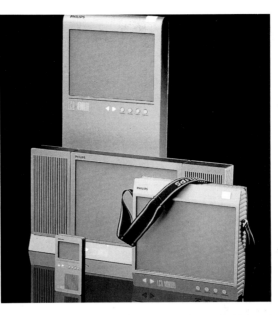

177-9. LCD (liquid crystal display) is a fast-developing technology, and these three products explore potential applications.

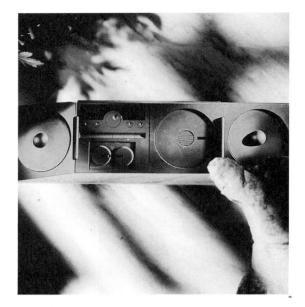

areas. Moreover, a global company needs to have its products universally available and identifiable, whether in small neighbourhood stories in any country or the international context of airport duty-free shops. A corollary of harmonization is the concept of a linked system rather than disparate products. This concept is evident in the Matchline system at one end of the market, and Moving Sound at another, or in PEOS and in Medical Systems. The development of a systems concept needs to me more than a change of name or exterior form. The establishment of real compatibility between the component elements of a system means penetrating beneath the skin, and building genuine co-operation between contributory disciplines involved in product development.

180. Portable audio projects developed for Philips by consultants McCoy and Fahnstrom.

Of great importance is the change in the perception of design within the company, from being a cost centre to being a profit centre, a resource that together with marketing and manufacturing can identify and create new possibilities for the company. The roller radio is an outstanding example of how design led the creation of a highly successful new product, that found a new market for Philips. The PEOS was a similar design initiative, as was the Tracer shaver as a youth product. This was achieved not through designers playing the role of artistic visionary, but by having their feet firmly on the ground of the present and projecting their ideas and experience into the future. The illustration that accompany this section show some of the ways in which Philips designers are looking at the

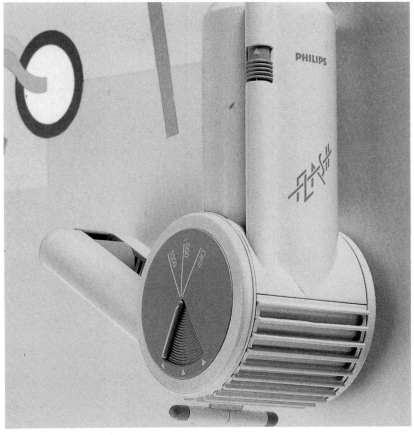

future from the informed standpoint of the present. The work on the Platinum project is an outstanding example of how a caring and informed designer established a close working relationship with other capable colleagues, researched his subject thoroughly, and made a fundamental contribution to a product that is several years ahead of the competition. The design management success in that story lies in the establishment of standards regarding an interdisciplinary approach in which design is an equal partner, in training designers to think in interdisciplinary terms, and in giving designers strong support and backing.

181-2. New develpments in personal care products include the two hair dryers (one fitted with a courtesy light) shown here.

183. The Glass Toaster uses flat foil technology in place of conventional elements.

The story is told in Philips that the development of the first dry shaver was an engineering initiative, initially disapproved of by mangement on the grounds that 'we are not the barbers of Europe'. The flexibility of attitude that led Philips to accept the dry shaver as a viable product, which has become one of the staples of its production, is equally as evident now and is just as necessary in a market climate of continuous challenge and change. The ability of designers to respond creatively to these demands can be a crucial element in the success of modern corporations. However, it requires a constant search for new solutions and the adaptation of new technologies in order to better satisfy user needs. Design management alone cannot ensure a flow of successful products, but by consciously creating a climate in which co-operation, interchange of ideas, stimulus and encouragement of creative innovation are part of the air designers breathe, it can significantly change attitudes and lay foundations on which to build long-term values and achievement.

184-5. New developments in lighting include both fixed devices and a series of rechargeable desk lights.

186-7. In-car audio and information systems in the Impact vehicle, a concept car developed with the British Company, International Automation Design.

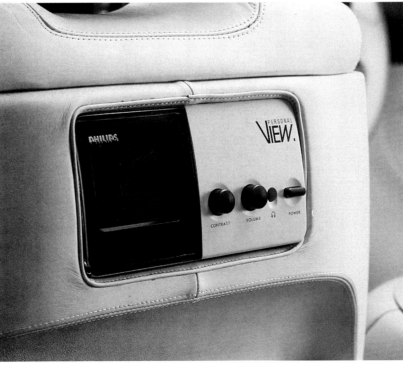

Index

Italics indicate pages on which
illustrations appear.